ISBN: 0-9826608-7-1
ISBN 13: 978-0-982-6608-7-4

MW00712798

You can visit us online at: *www.JacKrisPublishing.com*

Printed in the United States of America.

Ver. 1.0.0-1

Second Semester

Preface

We have designed this thorough program to be user friendly for both teacher and student. This program is arranged in **36 weekly lessons**. Lessons 19 through 36 are contained in this Second Semester book. Lessons 1-18 are contained in *Winning With Writing*, Level 6, First Semester book. Each lesson consists of five exercises labeled **Day 1** through **Day 5**.

Writing is very similar to other things in life; you need to have a plan and be well organized before you start. For example, you would never think of building a house without first having blueprints (plans) that clearly define the layout of the house. Without first having a plan, the house would certainly end up as a disconnected, unorganized mess.

In other words, you need to be organized before doing anything that is not obvious or simple. As I mentioned, being prepared before starting the actual drafting process is necessary. When writing we organize our writing by adhering to the following processes:

Outlining Process
1. The student first thinks of an idea (main topic) about which he wants to write.
2. The student then thinks of details that support his main topic. Instead of placing these details on a blank piece of paper, we provide a rough outline form when needed. This rough outline form is simply a place where general ideas are written in an organized manner. Completing the rough outline is the first step in organizing your writing.
3. After the student is through placing his ideas on the rough outline, it is used to build a final outline. It is during the transfer of information from the rough outline to the final outline that the details contained on the rough outline are further organized and developed into sentences for the actual writing assignment.

Drafting Process
1. The final outline is used as a guide to write a rough draft of the writing assignment. Typically, the student merely transfers the information contained on the final outline to the rough draft of the writing.
2. The student then edits the rough draft for grammar and content.
3. The final draft of the writing assignment is then written.

We believe this process is the easiest and most straight-forward way to write any type of writing. By using these processes, the difficult task of writing becomes extremely simple and easy for anyone. The processes taught in this book can be used for any type of writing of any length ranging from a single paragraph to an entire book.

Level 6 - Second Semester

Table of Contents

Student's Name: _____

Winning
With
Writing
Level 6

Second Semester

Date: _____

Types of Persuasive Writing

When writing we often try to persuade the reader by making statements of **fact** and **opinion**. A statement of **fact** tells something that can be proven, whereas a statement of **opinion** simply tells how somebody thinks or feels.

Fact: Susan is ten years old.

Opinion: Susan looks ten years old.

Obviously it can be proven whether or not Susan is ten years old. It might not be an easy thing to prove, but it can be proven. On the other hand, you can see by reading the opinion above that it is simply a statement about how someone feels.

It is important to be able to tell the difference between a fact and an opinion. Words like **think**, **believe**, **should**, **must**, **never**, **always**, **like**, **dislike**, **better**, **best**, **taste**, **beautiful**, **horrible**, **worst**, **seems**, and **probably** are all signal words that tell that an opinion might be present.

Keep in mind that no matter which words are used, if the statement can't be proven, it is a statement of opinion.

Also, whenever any **adjective** is used to tell what someone thinks or how they feel, it is a signal that an opinion might be present.

This car is really **long**.

This piece of wood is **old**.

That roller coaster moves **fast**.

A. Write an **F** for a <u>statement of **fact**</u> or an **O** for a <u>statement of **opinion**</u> for each sentence. If a statement of **fact** is present, rewrite it as a statement of **opinion**. If a statement of **opinion** is present, rewrite it as a statement of **fact**. It is fine to be creative with your sentences.

1. ____ I need to be at work by 9:00 a.m.

_____

2. ____ This couch is very uncomfortable.

_____

3. ____ The walk we went on was long.

_____

4. ____ My Dad is fifty years old.

_____

5. ____ That painting looks terrible.

_____

6. ____ I own a blue car and a red car.

_____

7. ____ Kevin Smith starred in the late night movie.

_____

8. ____ Bobby is a friendly boy.

_____

9. ____ Bonnie has five hundred dollars in her bank account.

_____

Date: _____

Types of Persuasive Writing

Often when we write to persuade, we make emotional appeals to the reader. An **emotional appeal** is used to play on the emotions of the reader in an attempt to get the reader to agree with the writer.

People have strong feelings or emotions about many things such as the environment, taxes, social programs, energy policies, child rearing, and the judicial system, just to name a few. An emotional appeal is one writer's attempt to express his feelings on a given topic in hopes of persuading others to share those same feelings. Please keep in mind there are at least two different opinions for every topic (supporting and opposing).

Below is one writer's emotional appeal to readers to help save the earth from impending environmental disaster.

It is our duty as citizens of this planet to keep it clean for our children and future generations. Mankind has been polluting our earth at an alarming rate for decades. It would be unthinkable for us to be so irresponsible that we pollute our water systems and atmosphere to the point that the earth becomes uninhabitable for future generations.

Here is another emotional appeal on the same topic, but it is supporting a different view.

Of course it is our duty to protect the earth, but the fact is that mankind has been steadily improving its behavior with respect to the environment for decades. The environment is cleaner now than it has ever been. This generation will leave the planet in excellent environmental condition.

A. Think about something you feel very strongly about and write a short paragraph. You do not have to do any outlining for this paragraph.

_____

_____

_____

_____

_____

_____

_____

_____

_____

_____

_____

_____

_____

_____

_____

_____

_____

_____

_____

_____

Date: _____

Types of Persuasive Writing

Another way a writer tries to persuade others is through advertisements. Advertisements usually use one or more of the following formats:

1) <u>Everybody's got one or everybody's doing it</u>

"Hi there, I have been using Suds-a-lot shampoo for many years, and so have all of my friends. It's the best shampoo in the world, and you should use it too."

2) <u>Famous people use it, do this, or have one</u>

"John Starshot can afford any walking shoes he wants, and he always chooses Fits-Right shoes for his walking needs. John says they are the best shoes anywhere. You too can look like a star if you wear them."

3) <u>Just ask this person who has done it or had one</u>

"If you don't believe me that Rocket Brand nose spray is the best, just ask George here. He has been using Rocket Brand nose spray for years and he loves it."

4) <u>Repeating something over and over</u>

"New Vision televisions are the best available. New Vision televisions have the best picture and the best sound. New Vision televisions represent the finest in viewing. New Vision televisions have the best warranty in the industry. When you need the finest, a New Vision television is the one you need."

A. Answer these questions.

1. Which method of advertising tries to lure the reader by telling them that someone famous uses their products?

   a. Everybody's got one or everybody's doing it

   b. Famous people use it, do this, or have one

   c. Just ask this person who has done it or had one

   d. Repeating something over and over

2. Which method of advertising repeats the product's name over and over?

   a. Everybody's got one or everybody's doing it

   b. Famous people use it, do this, or have one

   c. Just ask this person who has done it or had one

   d. Repeating something over and over

3. Which method of advertising wants you to ask someone who uses the product for their endorsement?

   a. Everybody's got one or everybody's doing it

   b. Famous people use it, do this, or have one

   c. Just ask this person who has done it or had one

   d. Repeating something over and over

4. Which method of advertising tells you that all of your friends have one of these products?

   a. Everybody's got one or everybody's doing it

   b. Famous people use it, do this, or have one

   c. Just ask this person who has done it or had one

   d. Repeating something over and over

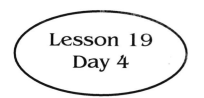

Types of Persuasive Writing

Date: _____

In this exercise you will learn how to write a **letter to the editor**. A letter to the editor is one that is directed to an editor of a magazine or newspaper. This type of letter expresses the opinion of the writer for almost anything that is on the writer's mind. When there is more than one persuasive reason in the letter, the least important persuasive reason is placed at the beginning of the letter, and the most important persuasive reason is placed towards the end. The following letter is a sample of a letter to the editor:

Dear Editor,

   I am writing today to express my displeasure with our city's efforts to keep others from illegally dumping trash throughout our community. I believe this constant cluttered look throughout most of our city makes it uninviting for potential visitors.

   I also believe the constant mess drives away potential new businesses and jobs from our community.

   Finally, I believe the constant clutter potentially attracts disease carrying rodents and insects that could harm the health of our community.

   We, as a community, need to take a collective stand against illegal dumping in our city.

Best regards,

Mrs. Debra Debris

The content of a letter to the editor is arranged similarly to other stories and letters. The content of the introductory and concluding paragraphs of a letter to the editor are slightly different than other types of stories/letters in that they explain their positions and try to persuade readers.

A. Answer each question.

1. What did Mrs. Debris feel was her best argument for cleaning up the city?

   a. The clutter drives away potential visitors.

   b. The clutter looks bad.

   c. The clutter attracts disease carrying rodents and insects.

   d. The clutter drives away potential new businesses.

2. What did Mrs. Debris want to do about the mess in the city?

   a. Take a collective stand against illegal dumping.

   b. She just wanted to bring it to the attention of the readers.

   c. She wants to clean up the city by herself.

   d. She wants the police to run a sting operation to catch illegal polluters.

Date: _____

Types of Persuasive Writing

A. Write either a **letter to the editor** or an **advertisement** in the style of your choice. Be creative!

_____

_____

_____

_____

_____

_____

_____

_____

_____

_____

_____

_____

_____

_____

_____

_____

_____

_____

_____

_____

_____

Date: _____

Thesis Statements and Transitional Sentences

A **thesis statement** is a one or two sentence summary of the main purpose or point of your entire writing. A thesis statement is similar to a topic sentence except that a thesis statement is a focused sentence for an entire writing, whereas a topic sentence is a summary for a single paragraph. The thesis statement is placed in the introductory paragraph.

- A thesis statement is **not** just a general statement.

Poor example: There are many great explorers in our history.

Good example: Louis and Clark were two great explorers of the early 1800s who explored the newly acquired Louisiana Purchase and points farther west.

- A thesis statement is **not** just a general announcement about your paper's subject.

Poor example: In this paper I will explain about early transportation in America.

Good example: One of the earliest mass transportation systems to carry people across America was the transcontinental railroad.

-and-

Poor example: My paper is about birds.

Good example: With its interesting eating techniques, the yellow-bellied sap sucker is one of my favorite birds.

- A thesis statement is **not** the title of your paper.

Poor example: American made cars are the best.

Good example: The quality of American cars has risen to a level that has never been seen in domestic manufacturing.

- A thesis statement is **not** a restatement of known facts.

Poor example: Sharks are known to swim in the ocean.

Good example: The great white shark is known to inhabit the South African coast and comes into contact with humans often.

A. Read each set of **thesis statements** and circle the best one from each pair.

1. a. This paper is about river rafting.

   b. Rafting on the Illinois River is fun but dangerous.

2. a. California has nice weather, but earthquakes are a constant worry.

   b. California has nice weather.

3. a. Airplane travel is safe.

   b. Airplane travel is statistically the safest way to travel.

4. a. The United States has had many great presidents.

   b. George Washington was a great president in our country's history.

5. a. Riding a bicycle is not only fun, but also a great way to stay healthy.

   b. Riding a bicycle is fun.

6. a. Juices that contain real fruit juices, vitamins, and antioxidants are healthy to drink.

   b. Juice flavored drinks are tasty.

Date: _____

Thesis Statements and Transitional Sentences

A. Write an **X** by the sentences below that are good examples of **thesis statements**.

1.____ The Grand Canyon is a deep hole in the ground.

2.____ Building a strong heart is one of the many reasons to eat healthy.

3.____ Although most houses seem similar on the outside, there are real differences in their structural quality when cities adopt building codes.

4.____ Beethoven was a great composer who had a profound impact on the world.

5.____ School uniforms are unnecessary.

6.____ Mistreated and abandoned pets are a growing concern among communities.

7.____ Deserts of North America seem similar on their surfaces, but in fact are very different from each other.

8.____ Studies show that educational television programming can have a positive impact on younger viewers' brains.

9.____ A pet cat can be very furry.

10.____ Dogs come in many different shapes and sizes, and with so much variety there is surely a perfect breed out there for you.

B. There are three sentences above that are **not** good examples of **thesis statements**. Rewrite each of the three and turn them into good examples of thesis statements.

1. _____

   _____

   _____

2. _____

   _____

   _____

3. _____

   _____

   _____

Date: _____

Thesis Statements and Transitional Sentences

A. Write a **thesis statement** for each idea below. Be creative and write about anything that is related to each idea. Writing a **focused** sentence is very important.

1. amusement parks

   _____
   _____
   _____
   _____

2. rivers

   _____
   _____
   _____
   _____

3. playing outside

   _____
   _____
   _____
   _____

4. a type of food

   _____
   _____
   _____
   _____

Date: _____

Thesis Statements and Transitional Sentences

Transitional sentences are the glue that holds independent pieces of writing together. Without transitional sentences, the writer is often left with disconnected thoughts that do not flow well from one paragraph to another.

A transitional sentence comes at the end of a paragraph and signals that a shift, contradiction, or elaboration will be coming in the following paragraph. Sometimes the first sentence of the next paragraph will also contain transition language which provides a link to the previous paragraph.

Transitions do not have to be lengthy or elaborate; in fact, a transition may only be a few words in length.

The following words are some examples of transitional words: **moreover, furthermore, finally, in addition (to), besides, therefore, consequently, thus, as a result of, for this reason, likewise, similarly, in the same way, in the same manner, however, nevertheless, in spite of, despite, in contrast, on the other hand, on the contrary, for example, in other words,** and **specifically.**

Below is an example of transitional sentences. The transitional sentences are in bold.

Birds migrate at different times of the year. When they migrate depends on how far north they live, and when their food supply disappears. Many birds migrate to where they can find food in the winter. Many birds follow mountain ranges, and many use the same flyway every year. **Some birds take flight for the winter; however, some of the heartier birds stay behind.**

There are birds that stay behind because they are easily able to adapt to the cold. Some birds eat seeds from dead plants, while others eat berries from bushes. Many birds huddle together for warmth, while some fluff up their feathers to trap air between the feathers to keep warm.

Can you see from the above example how the last sentence of the first paragraph is related to the first sentence of the second paragraph?

A. Read the paragraphs below and underline the **transitional sentences**. Remember that transitional sentences can also occur in the first sentence of the following paragraph.

There are many types of music in our world today. Although most forms of music sound very different, many types are played with the same types of musical instruments. Whether played at elevated levels or at a low mellow hush, music is a big part of most people's lives.

Pop music is usually played at an elevated volume. Pop music is usually performed with at least one electric guitar, one bass guitar, a drum set, and at least one vocalist. Pop music enjoys worldwide popularity and is especially enjoyed by today's youth; of course, most do not know that pop music is deeply rooted in rhythm and blues music.

Rhythm and blues music usually has a slower and steadier beat compared to pop music. The lyrics of rhythm and blues music are usually about the hard times of life or a lost love. Rhythm and blues is usually performed with an acoustic or electric guitar, an electric bass, a basic drum set, and one or more vocalists. Rhythm and blues is very popular throughout the United States; however, the same is true for country music.

Country music has grown in mass appeal in the past few decades. Country music has its roots with the American cowboy of the eighteen hundreds. In the past two hundred years, country music has spread to all corners of the globe. Music is almost unavoidable because it is everywhere.

No matter what type of music you enjoy, music is everywhere and has a soothing effect on its listeners. Music is meaningful, and where would we be without it?

Date: _____

Thesis Statements and Transitional Sentences

A. Write three pairs of sentences that have **transitions** linking the first to the second.

1. a. _____

   _____

   _____

   b. _____

   _____

   _____

2. a. _____

   _____

   _____

   b. _____

   _____

   _____

3. a. _____

   _____

   _____

   b. _____

   _____

   _____

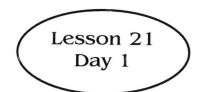

Date: _____

Persuasive Writing

A **persuasive writing** is structured very similarly to many other types of writings. However, the introductory and concluding paragraphs in a persuasive writing are a bit different from other writings in that 1) the introductory paragraph of a persuasive writing tries to convince the audience to agree with, believe in, or do what the writer wants, and 2) the writer uses the concluding paragraph to summarize his arguments made in the subtopics and to make one last plea to the reader to try and persuade him. The writer's best persuasive argument should be placed at the end of the body of the writing (the last subtopic).

Develop and write a **five** paragraph persuasive writing using the following writing process:

Outlining Process
  A. Complete the rough outline
  B. Complete the final outline

Drafting Process
  A. Complete the rough draft
  B. Edit the rough draft
  C. Complete the final draft

Make three persuasive arguments related to your main topic (your choices are below) that advance your position **for something** (one argument for each paragraph of the body of your writing).

Outlining Process

Write a persuasive writing **for something** by using one of the following main topics.

- Write a letter to the governor about laws on littering.

- Should children under the age of 16 be required to wear a helmet when riding a bike?

- Should pets be required to be on a leash when being walked?

After selecting your **main topic**, write it in the main topic section of the rough outline on the next page.

Date: _____

Persuasive Writing

The entire outlining process is explained in **Appendix B**. If you need help in completing the rough outline or the final outline, use Appendix B. Whether or not you use Appendix B, you still need to complete the rough outline and the final outline on the following pages.

Complete the rough outline

Rough Outline

Main Topic:

_____

_____

_____

Subtopic #1:_____

    Details: _____

    _____

    _____

Subtopic #2:_____

    Details:_____

    _____

    _____

Subtopic #3:_____

    Details:_____

    _____

    _____

Complete the final outline

Final Outline

Introductory Paragraph:

_____

_____

_____

_____

_____

Subtopic 1#:

   Topic Sentence:

_____

_____

_____

_____

   Detail Sentences:

_____

_____

_____

_____

_____

_____

_____

_____

Ending Sentence: (written after the topic sentence and detail sentences)

_____

_____

_____

_____

<u>Subtopic 2#</u>:

    Topic Sentence:

_____

_____

_____

_____

    Detail Sentences:

_____

_____

_____

_____

_____

_____

_____

    Ending Sentence: (written after the topic sentence and detail sentences)

_____

_____

_____

_____

<u>Subtopic 3#</u>:

    Topic Sentence:

_____

_____

_____

_____

Detail Sentences:

_____

_____

_____

_____

_____

_____

_____

_____

Ending Sentence: (written after the topic sentence and detail sentences)

_____

_____

_____

_____

Concluding Paragraph:

_____

_____

_____

_____

_____

Date: _____

Persuasive Writing

Drafting Process

<u>Complete the rough draft</u>

So far you have spent quite a bit of time filling out the rough outline and the final outline. As a result, your final outline has all of the necessary pieces to complete your writing.

If you think of something you want to add while you are writing your rough draft, please do so. The final outline will now be used as a guide to write a rough draft.

Start by writing your **introductory paragraph**, sentences for each **subtopic** (topic sentence, detail sentences, and ending sentence), and **concluding paragraph** on the lines below.

_____

_____

_____

_____

_____

_____

_____

_____

_____

_____

_____

_____

_____

_____

_____

_____

_____

_____

_____

Date: _____

Persuasive Writing

<u>Edit the rough draft</u>

It is now time to **edit** the rough draft you wrote on Day 3. Use the editing marks shown in **Appendix C** to correct any mistakes.

Do your paragraphs say what you want them to say? Do the words you chose make sense?

Look for and fix the following errors: 1) incorrectly used, misspelled, or misplaced words, 2) incorrect or missing spacing, 3) incorrect, missing, or misplaced punctuation, and 4) incorrect or missing capitalization.

Date: _____

Persuasive Writing

<u>Complete the final draft</u>

On Day 4 you edited your rough draft. Today you will rewrite your story in its final draft form.

Read your story one more time. Do your sentences flow well from one to the other? Does your entire writing make sense? Can you make it even better by adding 1) **time order words**, 2) **strong verbs**, 3) **adverbs**, 4) **exact nouns**, 5) **descriptive adjectives**, 6) **metaphors**, 7) **similes**, 8) **analogies**, 9) **personification**, 10) **hyperbole**, 11) **oxymoron**, 12) **alliteration**, or 13) **onomatopoeia**? Rewrite your edited paragraphs below.

_____

_____

_____

_____

_____

_____

_____

_____

_____

_____

_____

_____

_____

_____

_____

_____

_____

_____

_____

Date: _____

Persuasive Writing

Develop and write another **five** paragraph **persuasive writing** using the following writing process:

Outlining Process
    A. Complete the rough outline
    B. Complete the final outline

Drafting Process
    A. Complete the rough draft
    B. Edit the rough draft
    C. Complete the final draft

Make three persuasive arguments related to your main topic that advance your position **against something** (one argument for each paragraph of the body of your writing).

Outlining Process

Choose one of the following main topics and write a persuasive writing **against** the main topic you choose.

- painted graffiti on buildings and signs

- large people bullying smaller people

- smoking in public

After selecting your **main topic**, write it in the main topic section of the rough outline.

The entire outlining process is explained in **Appendix B**. If you need help in completing the rough outline or the final outline, use Appendix B. Whether or not you use Appendix B, you still need to complete the rough outline and the final outline on the following pages.

<u>Complete the rough outline</u>

<u>**Rough Outline**</u>

Main Topic:

_____

_____

_____

Subtopic #1:_____

      Details:_____

             _____

             _____

Subtopic #2:_____

      Details:_____

             _____

             _____

Subtopic #3:_____

      Details:_____

             _____

             _____

Date: _____

Persuasive Writing

Complete the final outline

Final Outline

Introductory Paragraph:

_____

_____

_____

_____

_____

Subtopic 1#:

Topic Sentence:

_____

_____

_____

_____

Detail Sentences:

_____

_____

_____

_____

_____

_____

_____

_____

Ending Sentence: (written after the topic sentence and detail sentences)

_____

_____

_____

_____

Subtopic 2#:

Topic Sentence:

_____

_____

_____

_____

Detail Sentences:

_____

_____

_____

_____

_____

_____

_____

_____

Ending Sentence: (written after the topic sentence and detail sentences)

_____

_____

_____

_____

Subtopic 3#:

Topic Sentence:

_____

_____

_____

_____

Detail Sentences:

_____

_____

_____

_____

_____

_____

_____

Ending Sentence: (written after the topic sentence and detail sentences)

_____

_____

_____

_____

Concluding Paragraph:

_____

_____

_____

_____

_____

Date: _____

Persuasive Writing

Drafting Process

Complete the rough draft

So far you have spent quite a bit of time filling out the rough outline and the final outline. As a result, your final outline has all of the necessary pieces to complete your writing.

If you think of something you want to add while you are writing your rough draft, please do so. The final outline will now be used as a guide to write a rough draft.

Start by writing your **introductory paragraph**, sentences for each **subtopic** (topic sentence, detail sentences, and ending sentence), and **concluding paragraph** on the lines below.

_____

_____

_____

_____

_____

_____

_____

_____

_____

_____

_____

_____

_____

_____

_____

_____

_____

Date: _____

Persuasive Writing

<u>Edit the rough draft</u>

It is now time to **edit** the rough draft you wrote on Day 3. Use the editing marks shown in **Appendix C** to correct any mistakes.

Do your paragraphs say what you want them to say? Do the words you chose make sense?

Look for and fix the following errors: 1) incorrectly used, misspelled, or misplaced words, 2) incorrect or missing spacing, 3) incorrect, missing, or misplaced punctuation, and 4) incorrect or missing capitalization.

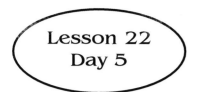
Persuasive Writing

Date: _____

<u>Complete the final draft</u>

On Day 4 you edited your rough draft. Today you will rewrite your story in its final draft form.

Read your writing one more time. Do your sentences flow well from one to the other? Does your entire story make sense? Can you make it even better by adding 1) **time order words**, 2) **strong verbs**, 3) **adverbs**, 4) **exact nouns**, 5) **descriptive adjectives**, 6) **metaphors**, 7) **similes**, 8) **analogies**, 9) **personification**, 10) **hyperbole**, 11) **oxymoron**, 12) **alliteration**, or 13) **onomatopoeia**? Rewrite your edited paragraphs below.

_____

_____

_____

_____

_____

_____

_____

_____

_____

_____

_____

_____

_____

_____

_____

_____

Date: _____

Compare and Contrast Essay

In this lesson you will draft a **five** paragraph **compare** and **contrast essay**. An essay is a truthful writing that is at least three paragraphs in length. Essays may be descriptive, use narration, or propose solutions to problems, but they are **not** fiction.

All essays have an introduction, a body, and a conclusion. In addition, essays are built around a thesis statement (see Lesson 20). As essay should be long enough to completely discuss, argue, prove, or relate the main idea of the essay (the thesis statement).

A compare and contrast essay takes two or more things and compares (tells how they are alike) and contrasts them (tells how they are different).

Develop and write a five paragraph compare and contrast essay using the following writing process:

Outlining Process
    A. Complete the rough outline
    B. Complete the final outline

Drafting Process
    A. Complete the rough draft
    B. Edit the rough draft
    C. Complete the final draft

Outlining Process

Choose one of the following main topics and write a compare and contrast essay:

- two different vacation locations

- living in the city or living in the country

- eating Mexican food or Italian food

After selecting your **main topic**, write it in the main topic section of the rough outline on the next page.

The entire outlining process is explained in **Appendix B**. If you need help in completing the rough outline or the final outline, use Appendix B. Whether or not you use Appendix B, you still need to complete the rough outline and the final outline on the following pages.

Complete the rough draft

Rough Outline

Main Topic:

_____

_____

_____

Subtopic #1:_____

    Details: _____

    _____

    _____

Subtopic #2:_____

    Details:_____

    _____

    _____

Subtopic #3:_____

    Details:_____

    _____

    _____

Compare and Contrast Essay

Date: _____

Complete the final outline

Final Outline

Introductory Paragraph:

_____

_____

_____

_____

Subtopic 1#:

Topic Sentence:

_____

_____

_____

_____

Detail Sentences:

_____

_____

_____

_____

_____

_____

_____

_____

_____

Ending Sentence: (written after the topic sentence and detail sentences)

_____

_____

_____

_____

Subtopic 2#:

Topic Sentence:

_____

_____

_____

_____

Detail Sentences:

_____

_____

_____

_____

_____

_____

_____

_____

Ending Sentence: (written after the topic sentence and detail sentences)

_____

_____

_____

_____

Subtopic 3#:

Topic Sentence:

_____

_____

_____

_____

Detail Sentences:

_____

_____

_____

_____

_____

_____

_____

_____

Ending Sentence: (written after the topic sentence and detail sentences)

_____

_____

_____

_____

Concluding Paragraph:

_____

_____

_____

_____

_____

Date: _____

Compare and Contrast Essay

Drafting Process

Complete the rough draft

So far you have spent quite a bit of time filling out the rough outline and the final outline. As a result, your final outline has all of the necessary pieces to complete your writing.

If you think of something you want to add while you are writing your rough draft, please do so. The final outline will now be used as a guide to write a rough draft.

Start by writing your **introductory paragraph**, sentences for each **subtopic** (topic sentence, detail sentences, and ending sentence), and **concluding paragraph** on the lines below.

_____

_____

_____

_____

_____

_____

_____

_____

_____

_____

_____

_____

_____

_____

_____

_____

_____

Date: _____

Compare and Contrast Essay

Edit the rough draft

It is now time to **edit** the rough draft you wrote on Day 3. Use the editing marks shown in **Appendix C** to correct any mistakes.

Do your paragraphs say what you want them to say? Do the words you chose make sense?

Look for and fix the following errors: 1) incorrectly used, misspelled, or misplaced words, 2) incorrect or missing spacing, 3) incorrect, missing, or misplaced punctuation, and 4) incorrect or missing capitalization.

Date: _____

Compare and Contrast Essay

Complete the final draft

    On Day 4 you edited your rough draft. Today you will rewrite your essay in its final draft form.

    Read your essay one more time. Do your sentences flow well from one to the other? Does your entire essay make sense? Can you make it even better by adding 1) **time order words**, 2) **strong verbs**, 3) **adverbs**, 4) **exact nouns**, 5) **descriptive adjectives**, 6) **metaphors**, 7) **similes**, 8) **analogies**, 9) **personification**, 10) **hyperbole**, 11) **oxymoron**, 12) **alliteration**, or 13) **onomatopoeia**? Rewrite your essay below.

_____

_____

_____

_____

_____

_____

_____

_____

_____

_____

_____

_____

_____

_____

_____

_____

_____

_____

_____

_____

_____

_____

_____

_____

_____

_____

_____

_____

_____

_____

_____

_____

_____

_____

_____

_____

_____

_____

_____

_____

_____

_____

_____

Level 6, Lesson 23 – Compare and Contrast Essay

Date: _____

Review of Types of Persuasive Writing

A. Write an **F** for a <u>statement of **fact**</u> or an <u>**O**</u> for a <u>statement of **opinion**</u> for each sentence. If a statement of **fact** is present, rewrite it as a similar statement of **opinion**. If a statement of **opinion** is present, rewrite it as a similar statement of **fact**. It's fine to be creative with your sentences.

1. ____   My sister is sixteen years old.

_____

2. ____   Those pants are ugly.

_____

3. ____   We have two dogs.

_____

4. ____   My mother is Christine Faskell.

_____

5. ____   These books are heavy.

_____

6. ____   I think this chair is comfortable.

_____

7. ____   I bought this shirt on sale.

_____

8. ____   Darren is a police officer.

_____

9. ____   We were late for class.

_____

Date: _____

Review of Thesis Statements

A. Read each set of **thesis statements** and circle the best one from each pair.

1. a. Red apples are delicious.

   b. There are many kinds of apples, but Jonathon apples are the best.

2. a. It snows in Alaska.

   b. The severe weather in Alaska can be deadly if you are not prepared.

3. a. The interstate roadway system in the United States is a marvel and was built decades ago.

   b. Roadways take us where we want to go.

4. a. This paper will talk about furniture.

   b. Modern furniture can be artwork with its intricate designs and bold colors.

5. a. Crops are food.

   b. A bountiful crop is necessary to feed the world's hungry.

6. a. Some milk comes from cows.

   b. Eating habits of cows affect the volume of nutrients in their milk.

7. a. The Eiffel Tower is in Paris.

   b. The Eiffel Tower was constructed in 1887 and was considered an eyesore by most Parisians.

8. a. We have had many great presidents in our history.

   b. Jimmy Carter was the 39th president of the United States, and he was also a successful peanut farmer from Plains, Georgia.

9. a. I will now tell you about paintings.

   b. Some of the most influential paintings were crafted centuries ago by Italian artists.

10. a. Basketball is a very strategic sport and requires superior team participation.

    b. Basketball is my favorite sport.

Date: _____

Review of Persuasive Writing

A. Answer these questions.

1. Where is the strongest **argument** placed in a persuasive writing?

   a. in the middle of the body

   b. towards the beginning of the body

   c. towards the end of the body

   d. in the greeting

2. What is a **persuasive writing**?

   a. a writing that tells about someone's life

   b. a writing that only presents facts

   c. a writing that tries to convince someone

   d. a writing that explains how to do something

B. What types of advertisements are the following?

1. "This is the best food in the world; if you don't believe me ask Terri here, she has been eating at our restaurant for years."

   a. repeat something over and over

   b. if you don't believe me, ask this person who uses it

   c. famous people use it

   d. everybody's got one or using it

2. "These ladders are the best available. Everyone has one and they love it."

   a. repeat something over and over

   b. if you don't believe me, ask this person who uses it

   c. famous people use it

   d. everybody's got one or using it

3. "This is Mr. Moviestar, and I only drink super energy drink."

   a. repeat something over and over

   b. if you don't believe me, ask this person who uses it

   c. famous people use it

   d. everybody's got one or using it

Date: _____

Review of
Persuasive Writing

A. Answer the following questions.

1. Place the below steps to writing a **persuasive writing** in the correct order.

   a. ___ Editing the Rough Draft

   b. ___ Completing the Rough Outline

   c. ___ Completing the Final Draft

   d. ___ Completing the Rough Draft

   e. ___ Completing the Final Outline

2. In which step does the author write the persuasive writing for the second time?

   a. Editing the Rough Draft
   b. Completing the Rough Outline
   c. Completing the Final Draft
   d. Completing the Rough Draft
   e. Completing the Final Outline

3. How are the introductory and concluding paragraphs different in a persuasive writing?

   a. They are actually the same as any other introductory or concluding paragraph.
   b. They try to convince the reader to agree with the writer.
   c. They are much shorter than ordinary introductory and concluding paragraphs.
   d. The introductory paragraph is longer and the concluding paragraph is shorter.

4. Which of the below are types of persuasive writing?

   a. ___ a narrative story

   b. ___ a letter to the editor

   c. ___ an advertisement

   d. ___ a descriptive story

Date: _____

Review of
Compare and Contrast
Essay

Information has been provided on the rough outline below. Use this information to complete the final outline on the next page.

Rough Outline

Main Topic:

Zoo animals

Subtopic #1: bears

> **Details**: meat eaters
> huge claws
> excellent hunters

Subtopic #2: lions

> **Details**: male lion is the head of pride
> female lions are the hunters
> excellent hunters

Subtopic #3: snakes

> **Details**: constrictors
> venomous snakes
> flying snakes

Final Outline

Introductory Paragraph:

_____

_____

_____

_____

_____

Subtopic 1#:

    Topic Sentence:

    _____

    _____

    _____

    _____

    Detail Sentences:

    _____

    _____

    _____

    _____

    _____

    _____

    _____

    _____

    Ending Sentence: (written after the topic sentence and detail sentences)

    _____

    _____

    _____

    _____

<u>**Subtopic 2#**</u>:

    Topic Sentence:

_____

_____

_____

_____

    Detail Sentences:

_____

_____

_____

_____

_____

_____

_____

    Ending Sentence: (written after the topic sentence and detail sentences)

_____

_____

_____

_____

<u>**Subtopic 3#**</u>:

    Topic Sentence:

_____

_____

_____

_____

Detail Sentences:

_____

_____

_____

_____

_____

_____

_____

Ending Sentence: (written after the topic sentence and detail sentences)

_____

_____

_____

_____

Concluding Paragraph:

_____

_____

_____

_____

_____

Documenting Sources

Date: _____

When writing, authors often integrate selected words from external sources into their writing to reinforce their position or to make a point. When bringing words from external sources into his writing, the author must signal to the reader that such words are not his and are in fact those of another. This is accomplished by entering a citation into the writing that integrates the external text.

A citation is a short piece of information that identifies the external source and tells the reader where he can locate the cited external materials. There are numerous different citation styles which have gathered support from various groups over the years, but for literary studies the citation style most accepted was developed by the Modern Language Association. There are different variations of the Modern Language Association format, so it is possible that other MLA citing sources might vary slightly from the examples in this lesson.

Why do we quote other authors? Perhaps the quoted author has stated something so perfectly that his statement would lose meaning or significance if it were reworded by the writer. Another reason to quote an author is if that author has expressed a point that is contrary to the writer's position or one that bolsters his position.

When a writer quotes another's work, the writer inserts an appropriate signal to credit the original author. This will be covered later in this lesson.

The last page of any written report should include a bibliography (works cited). A bibliography is a list of the sources used by the author of the report. The bibliography provides enough information to the reader to enable him to find the referenced external materials if desired.

A. Answer the questions below.

  1. Why do authors quote external sources?

    a. it is much easier than writing the words yourself

    b. because that author has already stated the point perfectly

    c. because you have to use external sources for most papers

    d. because quoting external sources makes your paper look more technical

2. Which citation style is most accepted by the literary community?

   a. *Publication Manual of the American Psychological Association*

   b. Turabian Citation Style

   c. the Modern Language Association format

   d. Chicago Citation Style

3. What is usually contained on the last page of a writing with quoted materials?

   a. a bibliography (works cited) page

   b. more quotes

   c. a summary of your writing

   d. a short biography on each quoted author

4. What is a quote?

   a. a statement of fact

   b. a question

   c. the actual words of someone else

   d. your actual words

Documenting Sources

Date: _____

So far we have learned that quotes are the external language of another person that are brought into someone else's writing. How exactly do we do this? The first thing we need to do is learn how to identify different types of external documents which are normally quoted.

On the next page are the cite formats with an example for each which shows how to quote various external sources. Of course almost anything can be quoted, but the examples given represent those that are most often quoted.

Let's assume that we want to quote some language from a fictitious book titled The Big Circus. It was written by George Post in 1998 and published by ABC Publishing, which is located in New York City, New York. The language we want to quote is on page 100 where the author talks about the dangers of walking the tight rope. How would we write a citation entry for our bibliography at the end of our paper?

We can see by looking below that the citation format for a book is as follows:

Author last name, first name. Title of Book. Place of Publication: Publisher, year of
    publication. Medium of Publication.

Most of the parts of this citation form are obvious except for the medium of publication. This part of the citation tells the reader where the cited words were found, such as **print** or **digital media**.

All we need to do to form a citation is to put the information we know about the book into this format. Our citation for The Big Circus would look like the following:

Post, George. The Big Circus. New York: ABC Publishing, 2006. Print.

This citation would be placed in the bibliography at the end of the writing. You will find more samples of external documents that are often quoted on the next two pages.

Magazine article

Author last name, first name. "Title of Article." Title of Periodical Day Month Year of publication: page numbers of the referenced article. Medium of publication.

Smith, Regina. "The Awesome Responsibility of Raising Children." Education Magazine 30 June 2011: 48-51. Print.

Book

Author last name, first name. Title of Book. Edition of book if not the first edition. Place of Publication: Publisher, year of publication. Medium of Publication.

Smith, Scott. Indiana's Lost Treasures. 3rd ed. Indianapolis: Historical Press, 2001. Print.

Encyclopedia (with more than one volume)

Author (if given) last name, first name. "Title of Article." Title of Encyclopedia. Edition. Place of publication: Year of publication. Volume number, page number.

Jones, Morris. "Volcanoes of the Pacific." Encyclopedia Britannica. Summer edition. 1992. Volume 16, 112-116.

Web site

Author last name, first name (if given). "Title of Article of Page." Title of site. Editor. (if there is one) Sponsor of Web site. Version number or publication date of article. Web site address (URL). Date of website access [There is no period at the end of a web site citation.]

Sherman, Chris. "Everything You Ever Wanted to Know About URL." SearchEngineWatch. Ed. Danny Sullivan. 24 Aug. 2004. 4 Sept. 2004 <http://searchenginewatch.com/searchday/article.php/3398511>

Interview You Conducted

Name of Person Interviewed. Personal Interview. Date of Interview.

Jones, Gary. Personal Interview. Dec. 1, 2010.

Pamphlets

Source of Info. Title. Place of Publication: Publisher, Date.

Office of the Head Coach. Playing to Win. Boston: University Press, 2005.

A. Given the information below, write correctly formatted citations.

1. **Book**:
   A book written by: Amery Hodnett
   Title: <u>Another Day, Another Dollar</u>
   Place of publication: Dayton, Ohio
   Publication date: December 2, 2008
   Publisher: Rothchild Publishers
   Medium of publication: Electronic Media

   _____

   _____

2. **Magazine Article**:
   An article written by: Bob Arnett
   Title of article: "Big Things to Come in the Automotive World"
   Title of periodical: <u>Cars Today</u>
   Publication date: October 24, 2009
   Page numbers of article: 12-15
   Medium of publication: Print

   _____

   _____

3. **Encyclopedia Article**:
   An article written by: Henry Smith
   Title of article: "Animals of the Forest"
   Title of publication: <u>ABC Encyclopedia</u>
   Edition: 3rd edition
   Publication date: February 20, 2010
   Volume number: Volume 3
   Page numbers of article: 102-112

   _____

   _____

Lesson 25
Day 3

Documenting Sources

Date: _____

So far we have learned to identify external sources that can be integrated into another document by quotation. We have also learned how to arrange quoted information into formats that are suitable for insertion into a bibliography.

All of this leads up to integrating another person's language into our document as a quote.

Let's assume we are writing an article entitled "Animals of the Forest." We have come across an article entitled "Rabbits in the Woods" that has the following paragraph with a sentence (underlined) that we want to include in our writing:

> Depending upon the time of year, rabbits are known to make a nest in the woods. As a matter of fact, many times you will find that <u>there are several species of rabbits that make their nests in the woods</u>. There are also many predators that the rabbits need to be aware of.

We will now demonstrate how to include this sentence into our writing. Below is the paragraph from **our** article (without the correct citation) that contains the quote from "Rabbits in the Woods" that we integrated into our paragraph:

> There are several animals that make their home year-round in the forest. At any given time <u>there are several species of rabbits that make their nests in the woods.</u> With this in mind we must be careful when walking through the woods.

The magazine article that contains the "Rabbits in the Woods" article was found in the following magazine:

Magazine Article:
An article written by: Tim Benovich
Title of article: "Rabbits in the Woods"
Title of publication: <u>Wild Animals Monthly</u>
Publication date: March 18, 2005
Page numbers of article: 20-23
Medium of publication: Electronic Media

Here is how our paragraph would look **with a correct citation** in our paragraph.

> There are several animals that make their home year-round in the forest. At any given time "there are several species of rabbits that make their nests in the woods" **(Benovich 23)**. With this in mind we must be careful when walking through the woods.

Notice that the actual quoted language has been placed in quotations in our paragraph.

Another way to cite the source is to include the author's name in the sentence. If Mr. Benovich's name was already included in the sentence, then his name would not have to be included along with the cite **(23)**. For example:

> There are several animals that make their home year-round in the forest. **Mr. Tim Benovich** stated that "there are several species of rabbits that make their nests in the woods" **(23)**. With this in mind we must be careful when walking through the woods.

Here is the corresponding citation that will need to be included into the bibliography at the end of our writing.

Benovich, Tim. "Rabbits in the Woods." <u>Wild Animals Monthly</u> 18 March 2005. Page 23 Print.

Notice that the second line of the above citation is indented five spaces. This is proper form for citations.

You can see how a connection is made between the small cite in our writing that integrates the language from Mr. Benovich's article, and the full citation of Mr. Benovich's article that was placed in our bibliography. MLA format follows the author-page method of in-text citation (the small cite in the actual text). This means that the author's last name and the page number(s) from which the quotation or paraphrase is taken must appear in the text, and a complete reference should appear in your bibliography (works cited) page. As explained above, the author's name may appear either in the sentence itself or in parentheses following the quotation or paraphrase, but the page number(s) should always appear in the parentheses and not in the text of your sentence.

A. Write an **X** by each citation that is written in correct form. Look carefully.

1. ___ **(magazine)**

Sain, Bill. "Fishing Blissfully." Fishing Monthly 30 June 2011. Print.

2. ___ **(book)**

Mason, Steve. Baseball Chronicles. California: Homerun Press, 2008. Print.

3. ___ **(encyclopedia)**

James, Michael. "Sunken Treasures of the Atlantic." Encyclopedia Britannica. 3 ed. 1992. Volume 23, 11-13.

4. ___ **(pamphlet)**

Office of the Dean. "Time Passes, Will You?" Miami: Sunshine Press, 2011.

**Lesson 25
Day 4**

**Documenting
Sources**

Date: _____

In the bibliography.

1. List cited works in alphabetical order of **author's last name**.

2. List cited works **without** an author alphabetically **by title**.

3. First line of each cited work begins at the left margin – all other lines of that cited work are indented five spaces.

4. When typing your list, double space your cited works.

A sample bibliography (works cited) is shown below. Notice how the entries are

alphabetized in accordance with steps 1 and 2 above.

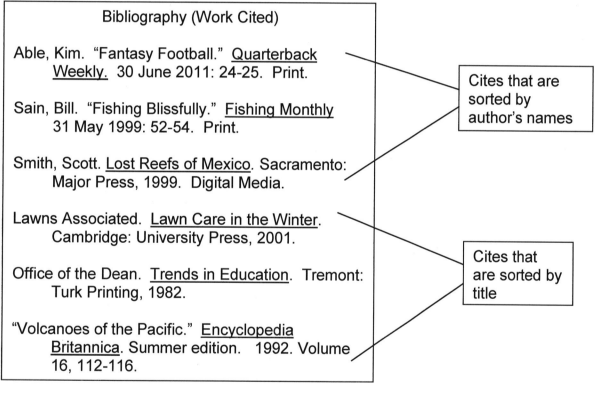

Bibliography (Work Cited)

Able, Kim. "Fantasy Football." Quarterback
Weekly. 30 June 2011: 24-25. Print.

Sain, Bill. "Fishing Blissfully." Fishing Monthly
31 May 1999: 52-54. Print.

Smith, Scott. Lost Reefs of Mexico. Sacramento:
Major Press, 1999. Digital Media.

Lawns Associated. Lawn Care in the Winter.
Cambridge: University Press, 2001.

Office of the Dean. Trends in Education. Tremont:
Turk Printing, 1982.

"Volcanoes of the Pacific." Encyclopedia
Britannica. Summer edition.   1992. Volume
16, 112-116.

Cites that are
sorted by
author's names

Cites that
are sorted by
title

A. What type of resource is each of the entries in the above bibliography (book, magazine article, pamphlet, or encyclopedia)? Look at the form of each to decide. Write the correct answers on the lines provided below.

1. _____

2. _____

3. _____

4. _____

5. _____

6. _____

Lesson 25
Day 5

Date: _____

Documenting Sources

A. Do some research and make bibliography entries of your own for each of the categories listed below. You can just make up information if you like as long as your form is correct.

book

_____

_____

_____

encyclopedia

_____

_____

_____

website

_____

_____

_____

magazine article

_____

_____

_____

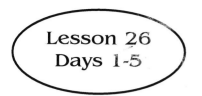

Date: _____

Cause and Effect Essay (Part 1)

In this lesson you will write a **five** paragraph **cause and effect essay**. A cause and effect essay gives reasons and explanations for things that cause an effect. There must be an immediate link between the cause and effect in order for a causal relationship to exist between the two. If the supposed cause is too far removed from the effect, then perhaps it is **not** a cause of the effect. For example, if you wash your hands and use a paper towel to dry your hands, the soiled paper towel is disposed into the trash. The trash is later burned, which could be a cause of air pollution. In this scenario, it would be difficult to say that washing your hands causes air pollution because that process is too far removed from the actual act of causing air pollution.

On the other hand, burning of the soiled paper towel could perhaps be a cause of air pollution since the burning actually sends pollutants into the air.

Let's assume that we want to write a cause and effect essay about **air pollution**. We would need to research various causes of air pollution such as vehicle emissions, factory smoke stacks, and forest fires. In our essay we would discuss the reasons and explanations of why we believe vehicle emissions, factory smoke stacks, and forest fires cause air pollution.

In this exercise, you will develop three causes for one of the **effects** listed on the next page of this lesson. Find and research **causes** for the chosen **effect** by going to the library, by using resources you already have, or by using the Internet. You will write one paragraph for each of your three causes.

Use the following writing process to build your cause and effect essay:

Outlining Process
    A. Complete the rough outline
    B. Complete the final outline

Drafting Process
    A. Complete the rough draft
    B. Edit the rough draft
    C. Complete the final draft

Outlining Process

When planning a cause and effect essay, begin by choosing the **effect** you would like to address. For this exercise choose one of the following **effects** for your essay:

1. noise pollution
2. global warming
3. high fuel prices

From this decision you will need to create a main topic. Write your **main topic** on the rough outline at the end of this lesson. In the outlining process you will use the main topic to develop a **thesis statement** (lesson 20). The following is an example thesis statement: "Noise pollution is a real problem in our major cities, and we must find a way to reduce it."

IMPORTANT! Before you start building your rough outline, the **effect** you chose from the above list will require some outside research. You will conduct this research to develop details for your rough outline. For this exercise you will develop three **causes** for the **effect** you selected.

For example, if you selected noise pollution as your effect, you could choose the following ideas as your causes: vehicle traffic, loud music, and construction. When building your rough outline, each of these causes would become its own **subtopic**.

Also, for this exercise you are asked to integrate at least **one quotation** into one of your subtopics (paragraphs). This means you will have to find one relevant resource to quote that is useful to your essay. At the end of your essay (in the final draft) you will also develop a Bibliography Page (works cited) that properly lists the reference(s) you cited.

Follow the schedule below to accomplish your assignment.

Day 1:
1) Complete the necessary research for your main topic. Add relevant details to each subtopic on the rough outline. Make sure the main topic is written on the rough outline.

Day 2:
1) Find one resource with a relevant quote for your essay.

2) Make sure to write your quoted language in the details section of the appropriate subtopic on the rough outline.

Day 3:
1) Make sure that the subtopics and details for each subtopic on the rough outline are complete.

Day 4:
1) By reviewing the rough outline, it should be easy to draft **topic sentences** for each subtopic on the final outline.

2) Use the details from the rough outline to develop **detail sentences** for each subtopic on the final outline. Write detail sentences (including the required quote) on the final outline in an order that makes sense for each subtopic.

3) Use the detail sentences for each subtopic to write **ending sentences** for each subtopic.

Day 5:
1) By reviewing the information contained in the entire rough outline, it should be fairly easy to draft a well-defined thesis statement. If a narrow **thesis statement** is not somewhat obvious, then perhaps you were too broad with the details that make up your subtopics. If this is the case, go back and further narrow your subtopics by focusing your thoughts more toward the main topic. The thesis statement will become a part of the introductory paragraph on the final outline. See Appendix B if you need help in writing the **introductory** and **concluding paragraphs**.

2) At the end of your essay you will need to develop a Bibliography Page (works cited) that properly lists the reference(s) you cited.

The **general** outlining process is explained in **Appendix B**. If you need help in completing the rough outline or the final outline, use Appendix B. Whether or not you use Appendix B, you still need to complete the rough outline and the final outline on the following pages.

<u>Complete the rough outline</u>

<u>Rough Outline</u>

Main Topic:

_____

_____

_____

Subtopic #1:_____

    Details: _____

_____

_____

Subtopic #2:_____

    Details:_____

_____

_____

Subtopic #3:_____

    Details:_____

_____

_____

Complete the final outline

Final Outline

Introductory Paragraph:

_____

_____

_____

_____

Subtopic 1#:

Topic Sentence:

_____

_____

_____

Detail Sentences:

_____

_____

_____

_____

_____

_____

_____

_____

Ending Sentence: (written after the topic sentence and detail sentences)

_____

_____

_____

Subtopic 2#:

Topic Sentence:

_____

_____

_____

_____

Detail Sentences:

_____

_____

_____

_____

_____

_____

_____

_____

Ending Sentence: (written after the topic sentence and detail sentences)

_____

_____

_____

_____

Subtopic 3#:

Topic Sentence:

_____

_____

_____

_____

Detail Sentences:

_____

_____

_____

_____

_____

_____

_____

Ending Sentence: (written after the topic sentence and detail sentences)

_____

_____

_____

_____

Concluding Paragraph:

_____

_____

_____

_____

_____

Lesson 27
Day 1

Cause and Effect Essay (Part 2)

Drafting Process

Complete the rough draft

So far you have spent quite a bit of time filling out the rough outline and the final outline. As a result, your final outline has all of the necessary pieces to complete your writing.

If you think of something you want to add while you are writing your rough draft, please do so. The final outline will now be used as a guide to write a rough draft.

Start by writing your **introductory paragraph**, sentences for each **subtopic** (topic sentence, detail sentences, and ending sentence), and **concluding paragraph**.

Introductory paragraph

You will start your essay by copying the information from the final outline to your writing. Start by transferring the **introductory paragraph** you wrote on the final outline, to the lines below. Read the introductory paragraph again to make sure it makes sense. Write a rough draft of your introductory paragraph. Remember to include your thesis statement.

_____

_____

_____

_____

_____

_____

_____

_____

_____

_____

Lesson 27
Day 2

Date: _____

Cause and Effect
Essay (Part 2)

Body

Next, you will transfer the information from the subtopic paragraphs. Start with subtopic #1 and work your way to subtopic #3. Write the topic sentence, detail sentences, and ending sentence for each subtopic. Write a rough draft of your subtopics (body) below.

_____

_____

_____

_____

_____

_____

_____

_____

_____

_____

_____

_____

_____

_____

_____

_____

_____

_____

_____

_____

_____

_____

Date: _____

Cause and Effect Essay (Part 2)

Concluding paragraph

Take the **concluding paragraph** from the final outline and transfer it below. Make sure your concluding paragraph makes sense. Write a rough draft of your concluding paragraph. You may also edit your concluding paragraph at this time (add or remove language, correct mistakes).

_____

_____

_____

_____

_____

_____

_____

_____

_____

_____

_____

_____

_____

_____

_____

_____

_____

_____

_____

_____

_____

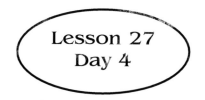
Date: _____

Cause and Effect
Essay (Part 2)

Assembling the rough draft

Now it is time to assemble the entire rough draft. Go back and read the pieces of your rough draft. Assemble your completed rough draft by 1) writing the rough draft of the **introductory paragraph**, 2) writing the rough draft of the **middle part** (body), and 3) adding the rough draft of the **concluding paragraph**.

_____

_____

_____

_____

_____

_____

_____

_____

_____

_____

_____

_____

_____

_____

_____

_____

_____

_____

_____

_____

_____

_____

_____

_____

_____

_____

_____

_____

_____

_____

_____

_____

_____

_____

_____

_____

_____

_____

_____

_____

_____

_____

_____

_____

_____

_____

_____

_____

_____

_____

_____

_____

_____

_____

_____

_____

_____

_____

_____

_____

_____

_____

_____

_____

_____

_____

_____

_____

_____

_____

_____

_____

_____

_____

_____

Date: _____

Cause and Effect Essay (Part 2)

Edit the rough draft

It is now time to **edit** the rough draft you wrote on Day 4. Use the editing marks shown in **Appendix C** to correct any mistakes.

Do your paragraphs say what you want them to say? Do the words you chose make sense?

Look for and fix the following errors: 1) incorrectly used, misspelled, or misplaced words, 2) incorrect or missing spacing, 3) incorrect, missing, or misplaced punctuation, and 4) incorrect or missing capitalization.

Complete the final draft

Today you will rewrite your paragraphs in their final draft form. Read your paragraphs one more time. Do your sentences flow well from one to the other? Does your entire story make sense? Can you make it even better by adding 1) **time order words**, 2) **strong verbs**, 3) **adverbs**, 4) **exact nouns**, 5) **descriptive adjectives**, 6) **metaphors**, 7) **similes**, 8) **analogies**, 9) **personification**, 10) **hyperbole**, 11) **oxymoron**, 12) **alliteration**, or 13) **onomatopoeia**? Rewrite your edited paragraphs below. Do not forget to include your bibliography at the end of this draft.

_____

_____

_____

_____

_____

_____

_____

_____

_____

_____

_____

_____

_____

_____

_____

_____

_____

_____

_____

_____

_____

_____

_____

_____

_____

_____

_____

Bibliography (works cited)

_____

_____

_____

_____

_____

_____

Date: _____

Biographical Essay (Part 1)

A biographical essay is a written story about a person. A biographical essay can include the history of the person as well as interesting stories (anecdotes) about the person. As the author, it is your duty to help readers see not only the life of this person, but also the reason this person was a significant part of history.

A good biographical essay might also include one or two unfavorable facts about this person. Was this person likeable? Was this person a hard worker? Was this person ever in trouble with the law? By adding both positive and some negative facts about the subject, the essay becomes more realistic and interesting to read.

Conduct some research to determine facts that make the subject of your essay significant enough to read about. For this exercise you will write a **five** paragraph **biographical essay**. You will need to find three significant facts about your subject. Research the person's background, life-altering events, and contributions to society. Take a lot of notes when you find quotable information about this person. Taking notes will help you identify and locate this information later when you cite these works in your essay. Go back and look at lesson 25 if you need help with citations.

Find these **facts** by going to the library, by using resources you already have, or by using the Internet. You will write one paragraph for each of your three facts.

In the introductory paragraph of the essay, discuss the subject's background such as the place of birth, date of birth, and life altering events.

In the body of the essay, you might want to start with a story, a quotation by or about the subject, or a compelling reason why you feel the subject is significant. After that, the material in the body is usually arranged in chronological order.

Conclude with a shorter discussion of why this person is significant.

Use the following writing process to build your biographical essay:

Outlining Process
    A. Complete the rough outline
    B. Complete the final outline

Drafting Process
    A. Complete the rough draft
    B. Editing the rough draft
    C. Complete the final draft

Outlining Process

For this exercise choose one of the following **subjects** for your essay:

1. Abraham Lincoln
2. Martin Luther King, Jr.
3. Mark Twain

  From this decision you will need to create a main topic. Write your **main topic** on the rough outline at the end of this lesson. In the outlining process you will use the main topic to develop a **thesis statement** (lesson 20). For example, look at the following thesis statement: Abraham Lincoln was not only a great president, but also a person who tried to right the wrongs of society.

  IMPORTANT! Before you start building your rough outline, the **subject** you chose from the list above will require some outside research. You will conduct this research to develop details for your rough outline. For this exercise you will develop three **facts** for the **subject** you selected. When building your rough outline, each of these facts will become its own **subtopic** (paragraph).

  Also, for this exercise you are asked to integrate at least **one** quotation into one of your subtopics (paragraphs). This means you will have to find one relevant resource to quote that is useful to your essay. At the end of your essay (in the final draft) you will also develop a Bibliography Page (works cited) that properly lists the reference(s) you cited.

Follow the schedule below to accomplish your assignment.

Day 1:
1) Complete the necessary research for your main topic. Add relevant details to each subtopic on the rough outline. Make sure the main topic is written on the rough outline.

Day 2:
1) Find one resource with a relevant quote for your essay.

2) Make sure to write your quoted language in the details section of the appropriate subtopic on the rough outline.

Day 3:
1) Make sure that the subtopics and details for each subtopic on the rough outline are complete.

Day 4:
1) By reviewing the rough outline, it should be easy to draft **topic sentences** for each subtopic on the final outline.

2) Use the details from the rough outline to develop **detail sentences** for each subtopic on the final outline. Write detail sentences (including the required quote) on the final outline in an order that makes sense for each subtopic.

3) Use the detail sentences for each subtopic to write **ending sentences** for each subtopic.

Day 5:
1) By reviewing the information contained in the entire rough outline, it should be fairly easy to draft a well-defined thesis statement. If a narrow **thesis statement** is not somewhat obvious, then perhaps you were too broad with the details that make up your subtopics. If this is the case, go back and further narrow your subtopics by focusing your thoughts more toward the main topic. The thesis statement will become a part of the introductory paragraph on the final outline. See Appendix B if you need help in writing the **introductory** and **concluding paragraphs**.

2) At the end of your essay you will need to develop a Bibliography Page (works cited) that properly lists the reference(s) you cited.

The **general** outlining process is explained in **Appendix B**. If you need help in completing the rough outline or the final outline, use Appendix B. Whether or not you use Appendix B, you still need to complete the rough outline and the final outline on the following pages.

Complete the rough outline

Rough Outline

Main Topic:

_____

_____

_____

Subtopic #1:_____

      Details: _____

              _____

              _____

Subtopic #2:_____

      Details:_____

              _____

              _____

Subtopic #3:_____

      Details:_____

              _____

              _____

Complete the final outline

Final Outline

Introductory Paragraph:

_____

_____

_____

_____

_____

Subtopic 1#:

Topic Sentence:

_____

_____

_____

Detail Sentences:

_____

_____

_____

_____

_____

_____

_____

_____

Ending Sentence: (written after the topic sentence and detail sentences)

_____

_____

Subtopic 2#:

Topic Sentence:

_____

_____

_____

_____

Detail Sentences:

_____

_____

_____

_____

_____

_____

_____

Ending Sentence: (written after the topic sentence and detail sentences)

_____

_____

_____

Subtopic 3#:

Topic Sentence:

_____

_____

_____

_____

Detail Sentences:

_____

_____

_____

_____

_____

_____

_____

Ending Sentence: (written after the topic sentence and detail sentences)

_____

_____

_____

_____

Concluding Paragraph:

_____

_____

_____

_____

_____

Biographical Essay (Part 2)

Date: _____

Drafting Process

Complete the rough draft

So far you have spent quite a bit of time filling out the rough outline and the final outline. As a result, your final outline has all of the necessary pieces to complete your writing.

If you think of something you want to add while you are writing your rough draft, please do so. The final outline will now be used as a guide to write a rough draft.

Start by writing your **introductory paragraph**, sentences for each **subtopic** (topic sentence, detail sentences, and ending sentence), and **concluding paragraph**.

Introductory paragraph

You will start your essay by copying the information from the final outline to your writing.

Start by transferring the **introductory paragraph** you wrote on the final outline, to the lines below. Read the introductory paragraph again to make sure it makes sense. Write a rough draft of your introductory paragraph. Remember to include your thesis statement.

_____

_____

_____

_____

_____

_____

_____

_____

Biographical
Essay (Part 2)

Date: _____

Body

Next, you will transfer the information from the subtopic paragraphs. Start with

subtopic #1 and work your way to subtopic #3. Write the topic sentence, detail

sentences, and ending sentence for each subtopic. Write a rough draft of your subtopics

(body) below.

_____

_____

_____

_____

_____

_____

_____

_____

_____

_____

_____

_____

_____

_____

_____

_____

_____

_____

_____

_____

_____

_____

Date: _____

Biographical Essay (Part 2)

Concluding paragraph

Take the **concluding paragraph** from the final outline and transfer it below. Make sure your concluding paragraph makes sense. Write a rough draft of your concluding paragraph. You may also edit your concluding paragraph at this time (add or remove language, correct mistakes).

_____

_____

_____

_____

_____

_____

_____

_____

_____

_____

_____

_____

_____

_____

_____

_____

_____

_____

_____

_____

_____

_____

_____

Date: _____

Biographical Essay (Part 2)

Assembling the rough draft

Now it is time to assemble the entire rough draft. Go back and read the pieces of your rough draft. Assemble your completed rough draft by 1) writing the rough draft of the **introductory paragraph**, 2) writing the rough draft of the **middle part** (body), and 3) adding the rough draft of the **concluding paragraph**.

_____

_____

_____

_____

_____

_____

_____

_____

_____

_____

_____

_____

_____

_____

_____

_____

_____

_____

_____

_____

_____

Date: _____

Biographical Essay (Part 2)

Edit the rough draft

It is now time to **edit** the rough draft you wrote on Day 4. Use the editing marks shown in **Appendix C** to correct any mistakes.

Do your paragraphs say what you want them to say? Do the words you chose make sense?

Look for and fix the following errors: 1) incorrectly used, misspelled, or misplaced words, 2) incorrect or missing spacing, 3) incorrect, missing, or misplaced punctuation, and 4) incorrect or missing capitalization.

Complete the final draft

Today you will rewrite your paragraphs in their final draft form. Read your paragraphs one more time. Do your sentences flow well from one to the other? Does your entire story make sense? Can you make it even better by adding 1) **time order words**, 2) **strong verbs**, 3) **adverbs**, 4) **exact nouns**, 5) **descriptive adjectives**, 6) **metaphors**, 7) **similes**, 8) **analogies**, 9) **personification**, 10) **hyperbole**, 11) **oxymoron**, 12) **alliteration**, or 13) **onomatopoeia**? Rewrite your edited paragraphs below. Do not forget to include your bibliography at the end of this draft.

_____

_____

_____

_____

_____

_____

_____

_____

_____

_____

_____

_____

_____

_____

_____

_____

_____

_____

_____

_____

_____

_____

_____

_____

_____

_____

_____

Bibliography (works cited)

_____

_____

_____

_____

_____

Date: _____

Review of Documenting Sources

A. Given the information below, write correctly formatted citations.

1. **Book**:
   A book written by: Lee Smith
   Title: <u>How to Throw a Fast Ball</u>
   Place of publication: Hopedale, Illinois
   Publisher: Rosti Publishers
   Publication date: 2005
   Medium of publication: Printed media

   _____

   _____

2. **Magazine Article**:
   An article written by: Ben Caragan
   Title of article: "What's Left for the Rest of Us?"
   Title of publication: <u>Economic National Register</u>
   Publication date: January 27, 2001
   Page numbers of article: 124-126
   Medium of publication: Digital media

   _____

   _____

3. **Encyclopedia Article**:
   An article written by: April August
   Title of article: "Geographic Oddities"
   Title of publication: Geography Encyclopedia
   Publication edition: 2nd edition
   Place of publication: Colorado
   Publication date: February 28, 2001
   Page numbers of article: 328-330

   _____

   _____

Date: _____

Review of Cause and Effect Essay

A. Assume you were asked to write a **cause and effect essay** on fuel shortages. Fuel (gasoline) shortages will be your **effect**, you are being asked to find three things that **cause** fuel shortages. Write your answers below.

1. _____
   _____

2. _____
   _____

3. _____
   _____

B. Turn the detail ideas from **part A** (that would have been written on the rough outline) into detail sentences that would be located on the final outline. Write your detail sentences below.

1. _____
   _____
   _____

2. _____
   _____
   _____

3. _____
   _____
   _____

Date: _____

Review of Cause and Effect Essay

Looking at the detail sentences you wrote for Day 2, let's assume that you read them again and felt that they could be made a bit better by inserting a citation for some quoted language. You went to the Internet or to your local library and found the following two pieces of information which you believed would be a good fit for your essay.

1. **Book**:
   A book written by: Harvey Ledbetter
   Title: <u>Gas Crisis Looming</u>
   Place of publication: Los Angeles
   Publisher: Deep Well Publishers
   Medium of publication: In print

   "With the recent population explosion during the past three decades, it has become very difficult for drilling and refining to keep up with world demand."

2. **Magazine Article**:
   An article written by: Gary Feinstein
   Title of article: "Is Our Fuel Almost Gone?"
   Title of publication: <u>Time</u>
   Publication date: March 13, 2009
   Page numbers of article: 87-90
   Medium of publication: In print

   "It has been reported that the world's oil supplies are dwindling, and by the year 2050 oil will become a scarce commodity."

A. Integrate the quotes from the previous page into two of the three detail sentences from **Day 2**, **Part B**. Rewrite all of the detail sentences below. Do not forget to place a proper citation when you rewrite the sentences. Also, complete the Bibliography (works cited) on the next page.

1. _____
   _____
   _____
   _____
   _____
   _____

2. _____
   _____
   _____
   _____
   _____
   _____

3. _____
   _____
   _____
   _____
   _____
   _____

Bibliography (works cited)

_____

_____

_____

_____

_____

_____

_____

_____

_____

_____

Lesson 30
Review
Day 4

Review of
Biographical Essay

Date: _____

A. A partial final outline relating to Wilbur and Orville Wright has been prepared for you below. Complete the introductory paragraph and the concluding paragraph. Remember to include a **thesis statement** in the introductory paragraph.

Final Outline

Introductory Paragraph:

_____

_____

_____

_____

_____

Subtopic 1#:

Topic Sentence:
-In 1878 the Wright brothers' father brought home a toy helicopter. This was the thing that sparked the boys' interest in flight.

Detail Sentences:
-The device was based on an invention of French aeronautical pioneer Alphonse Penaud.
- Made of paper, bamboo, and cork with a rubber band to twirl its rotor, it was about a foot long.
-"Wilbur and Orville played with it until it broke, and then built their own."   "Wright Brothers – Wikipedia, the free Encyclopedia" Wikipedia.org.
http://en.wikipedia.org/wiki/Wright_brothers

Ending Sentence:
It is interesting to find out how the Wright brothers became interested in flight.

Subtopic 2#:

Topic Sentence:
There were several people who actually flew aircraft before the Wright brothers.

Detail Sentences:
-In May of 1896, Samuel Langley successfully flew an unmanned steam powered model aircraft.
-In the summer of that year, Octave Chanute tested several gliders over the sand dunes along Lake Michigan.
-In 1899, Wilbur Wright wrote a letter to the Smithsonian Institute asking for information on aeronautics.

Ending Sentence:
-By seeing others fly gliders and unmanned aircraft, it caused the Wright brothers to become very interested in solving the problem of flight.

Subtopic 3#:

Topic Sentence:
The Wright brothers quickly understood that controlled flight would be necessary if safe flight were to be achieved.

Detail Sentences:
- In 1899, the hang gliding death of British flyer Percy Pilcher only reinforced the Wright brothers' opinion that "a reliable method of pilot control was the key to successful and safe flight." ["Wright Brothers – Wikipedia, the free Encyclopedia" Wikipedia.org. http://en.wikipedia.org/wiki/Wright_brothers] Up to that point, flyers in gliders would use the shifting of their body weight to balance and control the aircraft. The Wright brothers knew that there had to be a better way.
-Around 1901 the brothers experimented with various wing and rudder controls.
-In 1903 the brothers added power to their flying machine. Their first powered flight occurred on December 17, 1903.

Ending Sentence:
After two years of trial and error, on December 17, 1903, the Wright brothers had developed their controllable flying machine.

Concluding Paragraph:

_____

_____

_____

_____

_____

**Lesson 30
Review
Day 5**

Date: _____

| Review of
Biographical Essay |

A. Use the information from the final outline you completed on Day 4 of this lesson to write a rough draft of your biographical essay. Do not forget to make the correct citations for both quotations. You will **not** need to write a bibliography for this exercise.

_____

_____

_____

_____

_____

_____

_____

_____

_____

_____

_____

_____

_____

_____

_____

_____

_____

_____

_____

_____

_____

_____

_____

_____

Bias, Reliable Sources, and Taking Notes

Date: _____

Everyone has some sort of feeling or emotion that presents itself whenever they speak or write. This strong feeling is called a **bias**. This bias may be deserved or undeserved, correct or incorrect; nevertheless, this bias is simply how the speaker or writer feels about a topic. Sometimes a person expresses a bias even though he is unaware of it. Sometimes a person intentionally expresses a bias.

It is important for a reader to recognize bias when he sees it. Usually a bias occurs when the writer is stating his opinion with exaggerated claims rather than presenting his story with only facts. Another form of bias occurs when the writer presents only one side of the argument by stating only his point of view. Of course, most advertisements and some news stories contain bias.

A. Read each group of sentences below. If a group of sentences contains bias, rewrite the sentences to remove or negate the bias. One way to remove the bias is to remove the strong opinion or emotion of the speaker. Another way is to negate the bias by informing your audience that you are in fact reporting the bias of another (it is not your opinion). Act like you are a news reporter who is delivering a story that contains only facts or someone else's bias. There are no wrong answers in this exercise as long as you remove or negate the bias. The first one has been done for you. It's fine to modify the sentences slightly.

1. Mr. Mica's Steakhouse serves the best steaks in the entire state. Mr. Mica's steaks are aged at least 31 days for the best taste anywhere. You have got to try these steaks as they are simply the best.

   Mr. Mica's Steakhouse serves steaks. Mr. Mica's ages their steaks at least 31 days. According to Mike the owner, these steaks are simply the best.

2. I have a used car for sale that is the best car in the world. This car is a beautiful color of blue and only has 75,000 miles. This car is perfect for carrying 5 or fewer passengers. You can't go wrong for only $2,500.

   _____

   _____

   _____

   _____

3. Our neighbor's house is the most beautiful shade of yellow that I have ever seen. It has a grand archway over the ornate front door. The windows in the house are the most vivid pieces of stained glass that I have ever seen.

_____

_____

_____

_____

4. Our town has made at least ten unnecessary improvements to its major roads. Although our shattered roads were inadequate ten years ago, most have been upgraded to the point where they are fine now.

_____

_____

_____

_____

5. I saw a play last Friday that is one of the best I have ever seen. Brad Givens stars in the play as an energetic leader of a professional basketball team. This play lasts for ninety minutes and features the best ornate costumes and props. Mr. Givens deserves an award for his characterization of the story.

_____

_____

_____

_____

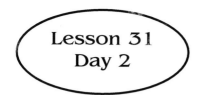

Date: _____

Bias, Reliable Sources, and Taking Notes

A. Write a paragraph on something you feel strongly about, like not being assigned homework over the weekend. Be sure to show bias in your writing. You do not have to perform outlining for this exercise.

_____

_____

_____

_____

_____

_____

_____

_____

_____

_____

_____

_____

_____

_____

_____

_____

_____

_____

_____

_____

_____

Bias, Reliable Sources, and Taking Notes

When looking for information, how do you know when the information you find is reliable? Of course some sources are always deemed reliable such as dictionaries, encyclopedias, almanacs, or other well-known sources.

One must always consider who is providing the information when trying to determine if a source is reliable and trustworthy. For example, would you have more confidence in information provided by a large corporation on its website, or information received from a small, recently established website from some unknown author? One would usually tend to find the information from the larger company more reliable.

You must also consider any bias of the author in the information. Is the information this person is providing slanted in any obvious way? Do some investigating to find out more about your source. Does this source have a history or reputation for taking extreme views on a particular subject? If so, you must keep this bias in mind when considering the views they express.

Depending on what kind of information you are seeking, your information might need to be extremely current. For example, if you are trying to write a story about a natural disaster that has occurred, sources of information you read today may no longer be current or reliable a day (or even an hour) later, as events can change quickly. In this case, even though the source may be reliable, the actual information you need may no longer be accurate.

A. Write an **X** on the lines of sources you would deem reliable for the given type of information sought.

1.___ You are writing a paper on the history of the Statue of Liberty. You have come across an Internet website that is hosted by the New York Port Authority that has facts about the statue.

2.___ You are to determine if schools in your area are adequately testing students. You have come across a blog from a parent who has children at the school. This parent shares her opinion on the school's testing criteria.

3.___ There has been a natural catastrophe and you want to write a current article on the events as they occur. You have found a radio channel that has a continuous live feed on conditions in the region. The radio channel is owned by a major news agency.

4.___ You are trying to figure out how to set up your Presto Print 900 printer. You have lost your instructions but have found a website that offers general information on how to set up a printer. You have never heard of this company.

5.___ You are seeking information to write an unbiased report on a war that is happening in a far away region. You have come across an unfamiliar magazine that features an article written by one of the leaders of the conflict.

6.___ You are searching for information about the amount of homework assigned at a particular school. You have in your possession a student newspaper from that school which has a student editorial stating that far too much homework is being assigned.

7.___ You are searching for information about the amount of homework assigned at a particular school. You have in your possession a written statement made by a teacher at that school who is known for giving students a lot of homework.

8.___ You are in the process of completing your taxes for the current year. Your next door neighbor offers tax advice. You know that he is a tax preparation expert at a local well-known tax preparation company.

9.___ You are seeking information about which automobile might be right for you to purchase. You happen to see an advertisement on a billboard from a local new car dealer which claims that the new Sunliner Extreme is the best car ever built at any price.

10.___ You are searching for information about the amount of homework assigned at a particular school. You have come across an article in the *Teacher's Monthly* magazine that describes the national guidelines for assigning homework.

Date: _____

Bias, Reliable Sources, and Taking Notes

A. Answer the below questions as to which type of source would be deemed most reliable for each given situation.

1. You need to find information about a specific type of purebred dog.

   a. an on-line internet site sponsored by an individual

   b. an article from the American Kennel Club

   c. advice you found in a flyer that was placed in your mailbox - you've never heard of the company that authored the flyer

   d. a friend who knows a lot about dogs

2. You are thinking about purchasing a new car and you would like to find information that compares models from different manufacturers.

   a. an article written by one of the car companies

   b. a non-biased report from Consumer Reports magazine that compared the types of cars you are thinking about purchasing

   c. an on-line website that has a chat room where people discuss a certain type of car that they already own

   d. a friend who knows a lot about cars

3. You heard a news story about a new highway being proposed that would run right through a local neighborhood. You would like to find a neutral party to provide only the facts as to why this highway should or should not be built.

   a. a person who lives in the neighborhood where the highway will be built

   b. taxpayers in the state who are being asked to pay for the new highway

   c. a next door neighbor who read an article in the local newspaper

   d. the commissioner for highways who has data showing that current traffic needs are overloading the roads and the new highway is needed

4. A young boy has been accused of stealing a piece of candy from a local grocery store. This matter has now gone to court and you are a juror in the case. You are searching for reliable information that will either prove or disprove the crime.

   a. testimony from the grocery store owner who was not present during the incident

   b. another child who was in the store at the same time the incident occurred - it is clear that this boy has never liked the accused

   c. a videotape taken by the grocery store's surveillance camera that clearly shows what happened

   d. the accused person's mother

5. You are an investor who sometimes lends money to people. You have been asked to loan Mike one hundred dollars. Before you make the loan you want to make sure that there is a decent chance that you will be paid back in accordance with the loan agreement between you and Mike. You want to make sure that Mike has a job and therefore will be able to pay back the loan.

   a. Mike brings you a current paystub (the part that is attached to your actual paycheck) which shows that he is employed at Slate Rock Quarry. The paystub indicates that Mike probably makes enough money to pay back the loan.

   b. You receive a telephone call from Mike's father who is a well-respected businessman in town. He tells you that indeed Mike does have a job.

   c. Mike promises you in a written statement that he is employed and will pay back the loan.

   d. Mike has one of his former employers call you to verify that he is a hard worker and is certain to find a job, if in fact he does not already have one.

Lesson 31 Day 5

Date: _____

Bias, Reliable Sources, and Taking Notes

Sometimes when gathering information, we need to quickly and efficiently record important information. One way to gather this information is to **take notes**. Taking notes can be done by writing each piece of information on a separate note card or by collectively writing them in a notebook. A notebook is probably the better choice since it tends to keep your notes together in one place and keeps them organized.

A note usually contains the three following important parts: a topic for the information being collected, the most important facts about the information, and a citation that will enable the information collector to find the source should that be necessary at a later time.

The following is an example of a **note**:

Black Bears

-good swimmers and tree climbers

-weigh an average of 125-600 lbs.

-eat mostly berries, nuts, grasses, and insect larvae

"The American Bear Association Home Page." The American Bear Association. 4 Sept. 2010 <http://www.americanbear.org/blackbearfacts.htm>

A. Find a source that gives facts about the **state** or **country** where you live. Quickly search this source and make **three** notes in the above format. Write your notes below.

1._____

_____

_____

_____

_____

2. _____

_____

_____

_____

_____

3. _____

_____

_____

_____

_____

Lesson 32
Days 1-5

Informative Essay
Research Report (Part 1)

In this lesson you will write a **five** paragraph **informative essay**. You will perform some research and report on the facts you uncover for the main topic you select from the list below. An informative essay is one that explains, describes, or gives information (**facts**) about **one** topic. An informative essay does **not** include the writer's opinion or try to cover multiple topics. The goal of a good **informative essay** is to provide the reader only with factual information.

Use the following writing process to build your informative essay:

Outlining Process
    A. Complete the rough outline
    B. Complete the final outline

Drafting Process
    A. Writing the Rough Draft
    B. Assembling the Rough Draft
    C. Editing the Rough Draft

Outlining Process

For this exercise choose one of the following **main topics** for your essay:

1. crazy laws that are still in existence
2. lesser known presidents of the United States
3. natural disasters

Write your **main topic** on the rough outline at the end of this day's lesson. In the outlining process you will use the main topic to develop a **thesis statement** (lesson 20). Look at the following example thesis statement: Almost every state in this country has laws that are old, outdated, and that have no place in modern society.

IMPORTANT! Before you start building your rough outline, the **main topic** you chose from the previous list will require some outside research. You will conduct this research to develop details for your rough outline. For this exercise you will develop three **facts** for the **main topic** you selected. When building your rough outline, each of these facts will become its own **subtopic** (paragraph).

Take a lot of notes when you find quotable information about your main topic. Taking notes will help you identify and locate this information later when you cite these works in your essay. Go back and look at lesson 25 if you need help with citations. Find these **facts** by going to the library, by using resources you already have, or by using the Internet.

Remember, this is not an explanatory writing where the writer explains the actual steps of how-to do something. Instead, this is an informative writing that tells the facts that the writer knows about a particular main topic.

In order to make informative writings more interesting, be sure to include **exciting adjectives** and **adverbs**.

Also, for this exercise you are asked to integrate at least one quotation into one of your subtopics (paragraphs). This means you will have to find one relevant resource to quote that is useful to your essay. At the end of your essay (in the final outline) you will also develop a Bibliography Page (works cited) that properly lists the reference(s) you cited.

Day 1:
1) Complete the necessary research for your main topic. Add relevant details to each subtopic on the rough outline. Make sure the main topic is written on the rough outline.

Day 2:
1) Find one resource with a relevant quote for your essay.

2) Make sure to also write your quoted language in the details section of the appropriate subtopic.

Day 3:
1) Make sure that the details for each subtopic are complete.

2) Develop an ending sentence for each subtopic.

Day 4:

1) By reviewing each subtopic, it should be easy to draft **topic sentences** for each subtopic on the final outline.

2) Use the details from the rough outline to develop **detail sentences** for the final outline. Write detail sentences (including the required quote) on the final outline in an order that makes sense for each subtopic.

3) By reviewing the information contained in the entire rough outline, it should be fairly easy to draft a well-defined thesis statement. If a narrow **thesis statement** is not somewhat obvious, then perhaps you were too broad with the details that make up your subtopics. If this is the case, go back and further narrow your subtopics by focusing your thoughts more toward the main topic. The thesis statement will become a part of the **introductory paragraph** on the final outline.

Day 5:
1) Write the introductory and concluding paragraphs on the final outline.

The **general** outlining process is explained in **Appendix B**. If you need help in completing the rough outline or the final outline, use Appendix B. Whether or not you use Appendix B, you still need to complete the rough outline and the final outline on the following pages.

Complete the rough outline

Rough Outline

Main Topic:

_____

_____

_____

Subtopic #1:_____

    Details:_____

        _____

        _____

Subtopic #2:_____

    Details:_____

        _____

        _____

Subtopic #3:_____

    Details:_____

        _____

        _____

Complete the final outline

Final Outline

Introductory Paragraph:

_____

_____

_____

_____

_____

Subtopic 1#:

Topic Sentence:

_____

_____

_____

_____

Detail Sentences:

_____

_____

_____

_____

_____

_____

_____

_____

Ending Sentence: (written after the topic sentence and detail sentences)

_____

_____

_____

Subtopic 2#:

Topic Sentence:

_____

_____

_____

_____

Detail Sentences:

_____

_____

_____

_____

_____

_____

_____

_____

Ending Sentence: (written after the topic sentence and detail sentences)

_____

_____

_____

_____

Subtopic 3#:

Topic Sentence:

_____

_____

_____

_____

Detail Sentences:

_____

_____

_____

_____

_____

_____

_____

_____

Ending Sentence: (written after the topic sentence and detail sentences)

_____

_____

_____

_____

Concluding Paragraph:

_____

_____

_____

_____

_____

**Lesson 33
Day 1**

Date: _____

Informative Essay
Research Report (Part 2)

Drafting Process

<u>Complete the rough draft</u>

So far you have spent quite a bit of time filling out the rough outline and the final outline. As a result, your final outline has all of the necessary pieces to complete your writing.

If you think of something you want to add while you are writing your rough draft, please do so. The final outline will now be used as a guide to write a rough draft.

Start by writing your **introductory paragraph**, sentences for each **subtopic** (topic sentence, detail sentences, and ending sentence), and **concluding paragraph**.

Introductory paragraph

You will start your essay by copying the information from the final outline to your writing. Start by transferring the **introductory paragraph** you wrote on the final outline, to the lines below. Read the introductory paragraph again to make sure it makes sense. Remember to include your thesis statement.

_____

_____

_____

_____

_____

_____

_____

_____

_____

_____

Date: _____

Informative Essay
Research Report (Part 2)

Body

Next, you will transfer the information from the subtopic paragraphs. Start with subtopic #1 and work your way to subtopic #3. Write the topic sentence, detail sentences, and ending sentence for each subtopic. Write a rough draft of your subtopics (body) below.

_____

_____

_____

_____

_____

_____

_____

_____

_____

_____

_____

_____

_____

_____

_____

_____

_____

_____

_____

_____

_____

_____

Date: _____

Informative Essay
Research Report (Part 2)

Concluding paragraph

Take the **concluding paragraph** from the final outline and transfer it below. Make sure your concluding paragraph makes sense. Write a rough draft of your concluding paragraph. You may also edit your concluding paragraph at this time (add or remove language, correct mistakes).

_____

_____

_____

_____

_____

_____

_____

_____

_____

_____

_____

_____

_____

_____

_____

_____

_____

_____

_____

_____

_____

Date: _____

Informative Essay
Research Report (Part 2)

Assembling the rough draft

Now it is time to assemble the entire rough draft. Go back and read the pieces of your rough draft. Assemble your completed rough draft by 1) writing the rough draft of the **introductory paragraph**, 2) writing the rough draft of the **middle part**, and 3) adding the rough draft of the **concluding paragraph**.

_____

_____

_____

_____

_____

_____

_____

_____

_____

_____

_____

_____

_____

_____

_____

_____

_____

_____

_____

_____

_____

_____

_____

Date: _____

Informative Essay
Research Report (Part 2)

Edit the rough draft

It is now time to **edit** the rough draft you wrote on Day 4. Use the editing marks shown in **Appendix C** to correct any mistakes.

Do your paragraphs say what you want them to say? Do the words you chose make sense?

Look for and fix the following errors: 1) incorrectly used, misspelled, or misplaced words, 2) incorrect or missing spacing, 3) incorrect, missing, or misplaced punctuation, and 4) incorrect or missing capitalization.

Complete the final draft

Today you will rewrite your paragraphs in their final draft form. Read your paragraphs one more time. Do your sentences flow well from one to the other? Does your entire story make sense? Can you make it even better by adding 1) **time order words**, 2) **strong verbs**, 3) **adverbs**, 4) **exact nouns**, 5) **descriptive adjectives**, 6) **metaphors**, 7) **similes**, 8) **analogies**, 9) **personification**, 10) **hyperbole**, 11) **oxymoron**, 12) **alliteration**, or 13) **onomatopoeia**? Rewrite your edited paragraphs below. Do not forget to include your bibliography at the end of this draft.

_____

_____

_____

_____

_____

_____

_____

_____

_____

_____

_____

_____

_____

_____

_____

_____

_____

_____

_____

_____

_____

_____

_____

_____

_____

_____

_____

Bibliography (works cited)

_____

_____

_____

_____

_____

Date: _____

Informative Essay
Research Report (Part 1)

In this lesson you will write another **five** paragraph **informative essay**. This time you will conduct some research about one of the inventions below. Your informative essay will provide facts about this invention. Remember, an informative essay does **not** include the writer's opinion or try to cover multiple topics. The goal of a good **informative essay** is to provide the reader only with factual information.

Use the following writing process to build your informative essay:

Outlining Process
    A. Complete the rough outline
    B. Complete the final outline

Drafting Process
    A. Complete the rough draft
    B. Edit the rough draft
    C. Complete the final draft

Outlining Process

For this exercise choose one of the following **main topics** for your essay:

1. mouse trap
2. hand-held flashlight
3. microwave oven

Write your **main topic** on the rough outline at the end of this day's lesson. In the outlining process you will use the main topic to develop a **thesis statement** (lesson 20). Look at the following example thesis statement: The origins of the common mouse trap are much more complex than most people realize.

IMPORTANT! Before you start building your rough outline, the **main topic** you chose from the previous list will require some outside research. You will conduct this research to develop details for your rough outline. For this exercise you will develop three **facts** for the **main topic** you selected. When building your rough outline, each of these facts will become its own **subtopic** (paragraph).

Take a lot of notes when you find quotable information about your main topic. Taking notes will help you identify and locate this information later when you cite these works in your essay. Go back and look at lesson 25 if you need help with citations. Find these **facts** by going to the library, by using resources you already have, or by using the Internet.

Remember, this is not an explanatory writing where the writer explains the actual steps of how-to do something. Instead, this is an informative writing that tells the facts that the writer knows about a particular main topic.

In order to make informative writings more interesting, be sure to include **exciting adjectives** and **adverbs**.

Also, for this exercise you are asked to integrate at least one quotation into one of your subtopics (paragraphs). This means you will have to find one relevant resource to quote that is useful to your essay. At the end of your essay (in the final draft) you will also develop a Bibliography Page (works cited) that properly lists the reference(s) you cited.

Follow the schedule below to accomplish your assignment:

Day 1:
1) Complete the necessary research for your main topic. Add relevant details to each subtopic on the rough outline. Make sure the main topic is written on the rough outline.

Day 2:
1) Find one resource with a relevant quote for your essay.

2) Make sure to write your quoted language in the details section of the appropriate subtopic on the rough outline.

Day 3:
1) Make sure that the subtopics and details for each subtopic on the rough outline are complete.

Day 4:

1) By reviewing the rough outline, it should be easy to draft **topic sentences** for each subtopic on the final outline.

2) Use the details from the rough outline to develop **detail sentences** for each subtopic on the final outline. Write detail sentences (including the required quote) on the final outline in an order that makes sense for each subtopic.

3) Use the detail sentences for each subtopic to write **ending sentences** for each subtopic.

Day 5:

1) By reviewing the information contained in the entire rough outline, it should be fairly easy to draft a well-defined thesis statement. If a narrow **thesis statement** is not somewhat obvious, then perhaps you were too broad with the details that make up your subtopics. If this is the case, go back and further narrow your subtopics by focusing your thoughts more toward the main topic. The thesis statement will become a part of the introductory paragraph on the final outline. See Appendix B if you need help in writing the **introductory** and **concluding paragraphs**.

2) At the end of your essay you will need to develop a Bibliography Page (works cited) that properly lists the reference(s) you cited.

The **general** outlining process is explained in **Appendix B**. If you need help in completing the rough outline or the final outline, use Appendix B. Whether or not you use Appendix B, you still need to complete the rough outline and the final outline on the following pages.

<u>Complete the rough draft</u>

Rough Outline

Main Topic:

_____

_____

_____

Subtopic #1:_____

    Details:_____

_____

_____

Subtopic #2:_____

    Details:_____

_____

_____

Subtopic #3:_____

    Details:_____

_____

_____

Complete the final outline

Final Outline

Introductory Paragraph:

_____

_____

_____

_____

_____

Subtopic #1:

Topic Sentence:

_____

_____

_____

_____

Detail Sentences:

_____

_____

_____

_____

_____

_____

_____

_____

_____

Ending Sentence: (written after the topic sentence and detail sentences)

_____

_____

_____

<u>Subtopic #2</u>:

Topic Sentence:

_____

_____

_____

_____

Detail Sentences:

_____

_____

_____

_____

_____

_____

_____

Ending Sentence: (written after the topic sentence and detail sentences)

_____

_____

_____

_____

Subtopic #3:

Topic Sentence:

_____

_____

_____

_____

Detail Sentences:

_____

_____

_____

_____

_____

_____

_____

_____

Ending Sentence: (written after the topic sentence and detail sentences)

_____

_____

_____

_____

Concluding Paragraph:

_____

_____

_____

_____

_____

Date: _____

Informative Essay
Research Report (Part 2)

Drafting Process

<u>Complete the rough draft</u>

So far you have spent quite a bit of time filling out the rough outline and the final outline. As a result, your final outline has all of the necessary pieces to complete your writing.

If you think of something you want to add while you are writing your rough draft, please do so. The final outline will now be used as a guide to write a rough draft.

Start by writing your **introductory paragraph**, sentences for each **subtopic** (topic sentence, detail sentences, and ending sentence), and **concluding paragraph**.

Introductory paragraph

You will start your essay by copying the information from the final outline to your writing. Start by transferring the **introductory paragraph** you wrote on the final outline, to the lines below. Read the introductory paragraph again to make sure it makes sense. Remember to include your thesis statement.

_____

_____

_____

_____

_____

_____

_____

_____

_____

Lesson 35
Day 2

Date: _____

Informative Essay
Research Report (Part 2)

Body

Next, you will transfer the information from the subtopic paragraphs. Start with subtopic #1 and work your way to subtopic #3. Write the topic sentence, detail sentences, and ending sentence for each subtopic. Write a rough draft of your subtopics (body) below.

_____

_____

_____

_____

_____

_____

_____

_____

_____

_____

_____

_____

_____

_____

_____

_____

_____

_____

_____

_____

_____

_____

_____

Date: _____

Informative Essay
Research Report (Part 2)

Concluding paragraph

Take the **concluding paragraph** from the final outline and transfer it below. Make sure your concluding paragraph makes sense. Write a rough draft of your concluding paragraph. You may also edit your concluding paragraph at this time (add or remove language, correct mistakes).

_____

_____

_____

_____

_____

_____

_____

_____

_____

_____

_____

_____

_____

_____

_____

_____

_____

_____

_____

_____

_____

_____

_____

Date: _____

Informative Essay
Research Report (Part 2)

Assembling the rough draft

Now it is time to assemble the entire rough draft. Go back and read the pieces of your rough draft. Assemble your completed rough draft by 1) writing the rough draft of the **introductory paragraph**, 2) writing the rough draft of the **middle part**, and 3) adding the rough draft of the **concluding paragraph**.

_____

_____

_____

_____

_____

_____

_____

_____

_____

_____

_____

_____

_____

_____

_____

_____

_____

_____

_____

_____

_____

_____

_____

Date: _____

Informative Essay
Research Report (Part 2)

Edit the rough draft

It is now time to **edit** the rough draft you wrote on Day 4. Use the editing marks shown in **Appendix C** to correct any mistakes.

Do your paragraphs say what you want them to say? Do the words you chose make sense?

Look for and fix the following errors: 1) incorrectly used, misspelled, or misplaced words, 2) incorrect or missing spacing, 3) incorrect, missing, or misplaced punctuation, and 4) incorrect or missing capitalization.

Complete the final draft

Today you will rewrite your paragraphs in their final draft form. Read your paragraphs one more time. Do your sentences flow well from one to the other? Does your entire story make sense? Can you make it even better by adding 1) **time order words**, 2) **strong verbs**, 3) **adverbs**, 4) **exact nouns**, 5) **descriptive adjectives**, 6) **metaphors**, 7) **similes**, 8) **analogies**, 9) **personification**, 10) **hyperbole**, 11) **oxymoron**, 12) **alliteration**, or 13) **onomatopoeia**? Rewrite your edited paragraphs below. Do not forget to include your bibliography at the end of this draft.

_____

_____

_____

_____

_____

_____

_____

_____

_____

_____

Bibliography (works cited)

Date: _____

Review of Bias, Reliable Sources, and Taking Notes

A. Write a paragraph on something you feel strongly about, like getting paid to help mow the lawn or work in the garden.

_____

_____

_____

_____

_____

_____

_____

_____

_____

_____

_____

_____

_____

_____

_____

_____

B. Find a source that gives facts about someone famous. Quickly search this source and make one note in the format shown in Lesson 31. Write your note below.

1. _____

_____

_____

_____

_____

_____

Review of Informative Essay

Date: _____

In this lesson you will write a **three** paragraph **informative essay**. You will perform some research and report on the facts you uncover for the main topic you select from the list below. An informative essay is one that explains, describes, or gives information (**facts**) about **one** topic. An informative essay does **not** include the writer's opinion or try to cover multiple topics. The goal of a good **informative essay** is to provide the reader only with factual information.

Use the following writing process to build your informative essay:

Outlining Process
    A. Complete the rough outline
    B. Complete the final outline

Drafting Process
    A. Complete the rough draft
    B. Edit the rough draft (not covered in this exercise)
    C. Complete the final draft (not covered in this exercise)

Outlining Process

For this exercise choose one of the following **main topics** for your essay:

1. electricity
2. snakes
3. rain

Write your **main topic** on the rough outline at the end of this day's lesson. In the outlining process you will use the main topic to develop a **thesis statement** (lesson 20). Look at the following example thesis statement: Electricity is perhaps the most important invention of modern man.

IMPORTANT! Before you start building your rough outline, the **main topic** you chose from the previous list will require some outside research. You will conduct this research to develop details for your rough outline. For this exercise you will develop one **fact** for the **main topic** you selected. When building your rough outline, the single facts will become your **subtopic** (paragraph).

Take a few notes when you find quotable information about your main topic. Taking notes will help you identify and locate this information later when you cite these works in your essay. Go back and look at lesson 25 if you need help with citations. Find these **facts** by going to the library, by using resources you already have, or by using the Internet.

Remember, this is not an explanatory writing where the writer explains the actual steps of how-to do something. Instead, this is an informative writing that tells the facts that the writer knows about main topic.

In order to make informative writings more interesting, be sure to include **exciting adjectives** and **adverbs**.

Also, for this exercise you are asked to integrate one quotation into your subtopic. This means you will have to find one relevant resource to quote that is useful to your essay. At the end of the concluding paragraph you will also develop a Bibliography Page (works cited) that properly lists the reference you cited.

Follow the schedule below to accomplish your assignment.

Day 2:
1) Complete the necessary research for your main topic. Add relevant details to each subtopic on the rough outline. Make sure the main topic is written on the rough outline.

2) Find one resource with a relevant quote for your essay.

3) Make sure to write your quoted language in the details section of the appropriate subtopic on the rough outline.

Day 3:
1) Make sure that the subtopics and details for each subtopic on the rough outline are complete.

Day 4:
1) By reviewing the rough outline, it should be easy to draft **topic sentences** for each subtopic on the final outline.
2) Use the details from the rough outline to develop **detail sentences** for each subtopic on the final outline. Write detail sentences (including the required quote) on the final outline in an order that makes sense for each subtopic.
3) Use the detail sentences for each subtopic to write **ending sentences** for each subtopic.

Day 5:
1) By reviewing the information contained in the entire rough outline, it should be fairly easy to draft a well-defined thesis statement. If a narrow **thesis statement** is not somewhat obvious, then perhaps you were too broad with the details that make up your subtopics. If this is the case, go back and further narrow your subtopics by focusing your thoughts more toward the main topic. The thesis statement will become a part of the introductory paragraph on the final outline. See Appendix B if you need help in writing the **introductory** and **concluding** paragraphs.

2) At the end of your essay you will need to develop a Bibliography Page (works cited) that properly lists the reference(s) you cited.

The **general** outlining process is explained in **Appendix B**. If you need help in completing the rough outline or the final outline, use Appendix B. Whether or not you use Appendix B, you still need to complete the rough outline and the final outline on the following pages.

<u>Complete the rough outline</u>

<u>Rough Outline</u>

Main Topic:

_____

Details:_____

_____

_____

Complete the final outline

Final Outline

Introductory Paragraph:

_____

_____

_____

Subtopic #1:

Topic Sentence:

_____

_____

_____

Detail Sentences:

_____

_____

_____

_____

Ending Sentence: (written after the topic sentence and detail sentences)

_____

_____

_____

Concluding Paragraph:

_____

_____

_____

_____

_____

Review of Informative Essay

Drafting Process

<u>Complete the rough draft</u>

So far you have spent quite a bit of time filling out the rough outline and the final outline. As a result, your final outline has all of the necessary pieces to complete your writing.

If you think of something you want to add while you are writing your rough draft, please do so. The final outline will now be used as a guide to write a rough draft.

Start by writing your **introductory paragraph**, sentences for your **subtopic** (topic sentence, detail sentences, and ending sentence), and **concluding paragraph**.

Introductory paragraph

You will start your essay by copying the information from the final outline to your writing. Start by transferring the **introductory paragraph** you wrote on the final outline, to the lines below. Read the introductory paragraph again to make sure it makes sense. Write a rough draft of your introductory paragraph. Make sure to include your thesis statement.

_____

_____

_____

_____

_____

_____

_____

_____

_____

_____

Date: _____

Review of Informative Essay

Body

Next, you will transfer the information from the subtopic paragraph. Write the topic sentence, detail sentences, and ending sentence for the subtopic. Write a rough draft of your subtopic (body) below.

_____

_____

_____

_____

_____

_____

_____

_____

_____

_____

_____

_____

_____

_____

Date: _____

Review of Informational Essay

Concluding paragraph

Take the **concluding paragraph** from the final outline and transfer it below. Make sure your concluding paragraph makes sense. Write a rough draft of your concluding paragraph. You may also edit your concluding paragraph at this time (add or remove language, correct mistakes). Make sure to complete the bibliography below.

_____

_____

_____

_____

_____

_____

_____

_____

_____

_____

_____

_____

_____

Bibliography (works cited)

_____

_____

_____

_____

_____

_____

Appendix A
Outlining Process
for a
Single Paragraph

The **writing process** actually has two parts, the **outlining process** and the **drafting process**. The outlining process is the **act of gathering information** necessary to complete a **rough outline** and a **final outline**. This appendix will explain only the outlining process. The drafting process will be covered in each individual lesson where it is needed.

As mentioned above, there are two items that need to be completed during the outlining process, the rough outline and the final outline.

Complete the rough outline

The outlining process starts by completing the rough outline. After the rough outline is complete, the information it contains will be used to develop a final outline. The final outline will then be used as a guide to write a rough draft of the paragraph. Below is a sample rough outline that shows its parts.

Rough Outline

- Main Topic
    - o Detail #1: (used to make detail sentences
    - o Detail #2: on the final outline)
    - o Detail #3:

> May be more or fewer than three

Step #1 (develop a main topic for the rough outline)

The first piece of information needed to complete the rough outline is a **main topic**. A main topic is a **very general idea** that tells what a paragraph is about. For example, let's assume we have decided that we want to write a paragraph about **arctic animals**. This bolded phrase is called the **main topic** of the paragraph. Notice that we called this a phrase and not a sentence. A main topic does not have to be a complete sentence. It only needs to be a very general **idea** for your paragraph.

A. When you decide on a main topic, write it in the **main topic** section of your rough outline.

Step #2 (develop details for the rough outline)

   Now that we have a main topic (the sample is **arctic animals)**, we need to think of **details** to complete the rough outline. A detail is a thought, phrase, or sentence that gives more information about the main topic. These details will be turned into **detail sentences** for the **final outline**.

   Assume we possess no knowledge of our example main topic arctic animals, so we conducted some research to gather information from the library, Internet, and some other dependable sources. Our research returned the following **details** about arctic animals:

   1. polar bears
   2. seals
   3. orcas

   These are **details** because they provide more description to the main topic of **arctic animals**.

B. Think of a few details for your main topic and write them under the **details** portion of the rough outline. With the addition of your **details**, the rough outline is complete.

Complete the final outline

   The next step in organizing our paragraph is completing a final outline that has the following structure:

- Topic sentence:
- Detail Sentence #1: (constructed from the main
- Detail Sentence #2:   topic and details in the
- Detail Sentence #3:   rough outline)
- Ending sentence:
       (restates the topic sentence and/or summarizes the detail sentences)

May be more or
fewer than three

Step #1 (write a topic sentence)

The first step to completing a final outline is writing a **topic sentence**. A topic sentence tells **generally** what the paragraph is about, but it does not provide specific detail about the paragraph. Its primary purpose is to get the attention of the reader.

By looking at the **main topic** and **details** written on the rough outline, we can use them to think of a **topic sentence** for the final outline. While the main topic in the rough outline may or may not be a complete sentence, the topic sentence in the final outline **must** be a complete sentence. Using our example main topic of **arctic animals**, our topic sentence could be something like the following sentence: **Arctic animals survive very well in the extreme cold**.

Step #2 (writing detail sentences)

The next piece of information needed to build the final outline is detail sentences. Detail sentences will make up the greatest portion of your writing. They actually tell the story of the paragraph. This makes the detail sentences arguably the most important part of the writing.

Look at the **details** written on the rough outline. It is our goal to use these **details** along with the **main topic** and **topic sentence** to think of interesting detail sentences for the paragraph. While you are thinking of these **detail sentences**, remember that they will all need to fit together as a paragraph. By the time you are done you should have several detail sentences written under the **detail sentences** section of the final outline. Make sure to place the detail sentences in the correct order if there is a required order for your writing.

Since you now have all of the information you need to think of detail sentences, write your detail sentences in the detail sentences section of the final outline.

After looking at our details, main topic, and topic sentence from our example (arctic animals), we added some detail sentences to our final outline. Our final outline now looks like this:

<u>Final Outline</u>

Topic Sentence:

   Arctic animals survive very well in the extreme cold.

Detail Sentences:

- Polar bears have a thick, furry coat which acts as a barrier to the cold.
- Seals have a thick layer of blubber and skin that protects them from the cold.
- Orcas can survive in cold water because they have a thick layer of blubber over their body.

Ending Sentence:

   (not developed yet)

Step #3 (writing an ending sentence)

   The last step to completing the final outline is to create an **ending sentence**. It is the function of the ending sentence to restate the topic sentence or summarize the detail sentences. For our example above, we could write the following ending sentence:

   "As you can see, most arctic animals that survive the cold have blubber or some kind of insulation."

   Create an ending sentence for your paragraph and write it on the **ending sentence** section of your final outline. With the addition of the ending sentence, your final outline is complete.

Appendix B
Outlining Process
for
Multiple Paragraphs

The **writing process** actually has two parts, the **outlining process** and the **drafting process**. The outlining process is the **act of gathering information** necessary to complete a **rough outline** and a **final outline**. This appendix will explain only the outlining process. The drafting process will be covered in each individual lesson where it is needed.

As mentioned above, there are two items that need to be completed during the outlining process, the rough outline and the final outline.

You will notice that the outlining process for writings with multiple paragraphs is a bit different than the outlining process for a single paragraph. Here are the differences between the two:

1. When multiple paragraphs are required in a writing, they are essentially grouped together to form a larger story or writing. When we have a single paragraph, the reader relies on its topic sentence to tell what the following paragraph is about. In comparison, when multiple paragraphs are grouped together, there is no such sentence or paragraph present that introduces the **entire** writing. Each individual paragraph has its own topic sentence, but none of the topic sentences introduce **all** of the paragraphs. Therefore, when multiple paragraphs are present there needs to be a separate paragraph to introduce or explain **all** of the paragraphs that will be in the writing. This paragraph is called an **introductory paragraph**.

2. The same can be said for a paragraph that concludes the entire writing. Each individual paragraph has an ending sentence, but there is no sentence or paragraph that summarizes the **entire** writing. Therefore, when multiple paragraphs are present there needs to be a separate paragraph to conclude the entire writing. This paragraph is called the **concluding paragraph**.

3. Since many paragraphs are being grouped together, the writer needs a way to identify each paragraph within the writing. The way this is accomplished is by numbering each paragraph as a subtopic. If you look closely at the rough outline or the final outline of a writing with multiple paragraphs, you will see that a subtopic is simply the same thing as a main topic. Of course each subtopic represents a separate paragraph within the writing. As you can see, each numbered subtopic still contains a topic sentence, detail sentences, and an ending sentence.

- - - - -

We will now start the task of completing the outlining process.

Complete the rough outline

The outlining process starts by completing the rough outline. After the rough outline is complete, the information it contains will be used to develop a final outline. The final outline will then be used as a guide to write a rough draft of the multi-paragraph story/writing.

Step #1 (develop a main topic for the rough outline)

The first piece of information needed to complete the rough outline is a **main topic**. A main topic is a **very general idea** that tells what the story is about. For example, let's assume we have decided that we want to write a story about **arctic animals**. This bolded phrase is called the **main topic** of the story. Notice that we called this a phrase and not a sentence? A main topic does not have to be a sentence. A main topic is a very general **idea** for your writing.

A. When you decide on a main topic for your writing, write it in the **main topic** section of your rough outline for the appropriate lesson. On the next page is a sample rough outline for stories/writings with multiple paragraphs.

<u>Rough Outline</u>

- Main Topic

- Subtopic #1:
- Detail #1: (used to make detail
- Detail #2: sentences on the final
- Detail #3: outline)

> May be more or fewer than three

- Subtopic #2:
- Detail #1:
- Detail #2:
- Detail #3:

- Subtopic #3:
- Detail #1:
- Detail #2:
- Detail #3:

Step #2 (developing subtopics for the rough outline)

Your writing will be comprised of one **introductory paragraph**, two or more paragraphs that form the middle part or **body**, and one **concluding paragraph**. This means that you will have to separate your writing into three pieces (introductory paragraph, body, and concluding paragraph).

Since the **body** of your writing will be made up of more than one paragraph, you must develop a **subtopic** (main topic) for each paragraph. Of course this means that each **subtopic** will represent a paragraph in your writing. For our sample story, we have selected three subtopics (your assignment may have more or fewer subtopics) which means that there will be three paragraphs that form the body of our writing.

After adding a **main topic** and **subtopics**, here is how the rough outline for our sample story looks so far:

Main Topic: arctic animals
Subtopic #1: polar bears
      Details: (not yet developed)
Subtopic #2: seals
      Details: (not yet developed)
Subtopic #3: orcas
      Details: (not yet developed)

A. Write the required number of subtopics on the rough outline for your writing. Make sure you write them in the correct order when they occur in your story (if a correct order is necessary).

Step #3 (developing **details** for the rough outline)
    Now that you have developed a main topic and your subtopics, you will next need to develop **details** to complete the rough outline. A detail can be a thought, phrase, or sentence that gives more information about the subtopic. These details will later be turned into **detail sentences** for the **final outline**.

    Assume that we possess no knowledge of our example main topic arctic animals. With this in mind, we conducted some research to gather information from the library, Internet, and some other dependable sources.

For our sample writing we came up with the following **details** for each subtopic:

Main Topic: arctic animals

Subtopic #1: polar bears
Detail #1: **white fur**
Detail #2: **blubber**
Detail #3: **powerful**

Subtopic #2: seals
Detail #1: **fur**
Detail #2: **thick blubber**
Detail #3: **fast swimmer**

Subtopic #3: orcas
Detail #1: **blubber**
Detail #2: **fast swimmer**
Detail #3: **top of food chain**

Our rough outline is now complete. You can see that by adding details to the rough outline the story is starting to become clearer.

B. Think of a few details for each subtopic in your writing and add them under the appropriate **detail** sections of your rough outline. With the addition of your **details**, your rough outline is complete.

Complete the final outline

You will notice that the rough outline and the final outline **both** have numbered **subtopics** (subtopic #1, subtopic #2, and subtopic #3 in our example) and **details**. The information contained in subtopic #1 in the rough outline (including the details) is used to build subtopic #1 on the final outline, and so on.

We will now start constructing our final outline which has the following structure:

Final Outline

- Introductory Paragraph: (introduces the entire writing)

- Subtopic #1: (can be as many subtopics as necessary)
  - o Topic Sentence: (tells about the paragraph)
  - o Detail Sentence #1: (constructed from the main
  - o Detail Sentence #2: topic and details in the
  - o Detail Sentence #3: rough outline)
  - o Ending Sentence: (restates the topic sentence or summarizes the detail sentences.)

  > May be more or fewer than three

- Subtopic #2:
  - o Topic Sentence:
  - o Detail Sentence #1:
  - o Detail Sentence #2:
  - o Detail Sentence #3:
  - o Ending Sentence:

- Subtopic #3:
  - o Topic Sentence:
  - o Detail Sentence #1:
  - o Detail Sentence #2:
  - o Detail Sentence #3:
  - o Ending Sentence:

- Concluding Paragraph: (summarizes the entire writing)

Step #1 (writing topic sentences)

The first step to complete the final outline is writing **topic sentences** for each subtopic. A topic sentence (the same thing as a main topic for a single paragraph) tells **generally** what the paragraph that follows is about, but it does not provide specific detail about the writing. Its primary purpose is to get the attention of the reader.

By looking at the **subtopics** and **details** written on the **rough outline**, we can use them to think of **topic sentences** for each **subtopic** in the final outline. While the subtopics on the **rough outline** may not be complete sentences, each **topic sentence** on the final outline must be a complete sentence.

A. For each subtopic on your rough outline, write a **topic sentence** in the appropriate **subtopic** section of the **final outline**.

If you would like to see the subtopic sentences we wrote for our sample writing, go to the end of this appendix.

Step #2 (writing detail sentences)

The next piece of information needed to build the final outline is detail sentences. Detail sentences will make up the greatest portion of your writing. They actually tell the story of the writing (each paragraph). This makes the detail sentences the most important part of the writing.

Look at the **details** written on the rough outline. It is our goal to use these **details**, along with the **topic sentences** you just wrote in the subtopics sections of the final outline, to think of interesting detail sentences for each **subtopic** (paragraph) in the final outline. While you are thinking of these **detail sentences**, remember that they will all need to fit together as paragraphs. By the time you are done you should have several detail sentences written under the **detail sentences** sections of the final outline. Make sure to place the detail sentences in the correct order for each paragraph if there is a required order for your writing.

B. Since you now have all of the information you need to develop detail sentences, write your detail sentences in the appropriate **detail sentence** sections of the final outline.

Step #3 (write ending sentences)

The next step to complete the final outline is to create an **ending sentence** for each subtopic. It is the function of each ending sentence to restate the subtopic or summarize the detail sentences of that particular paragraph. If you would like to see the ending sentences for our sample, go to the end of this appendix.

C. Write your ending sentences in the appropriate **Ending sentence** sections of the final outline.

Step #4 (write introductory and concluding paragraphs)

The **introductory paragraph** sets the stage for the rest of the writing. This paragraph may introduce characters or provide other information the reader needs to know to understand the writing as a whole.

*The paragraph applies **only** to essays:*

By reviewing the information contained in the entire rough outline, it should be fairly easy to draft a well-defined thesis statement. If a narrow **thesis statement** is not obvious from reviewing the rough outline, then perhaps you were too broad with the details that make up your subtopics. If this is the case, go back and further narrow your subtopics in the rough outline by focusing your thoughts more toward the main topic. The thesis statement will become a part of the **introductory paragraph** in the final outline.

Of course the introductory paragraph may also act to summarize the **subtopics** that follow.

D. Write an introductory paragraph in the **introductory paragraph** section of the final outline.

The last paragraph is the **concluding paragraph**. A concluding paragraph is used to summarize the entire writing. It may also be used to tell the ending of what you are writing.

E. Write a **concluding paragraph** in the concluding paragraph section of the final outline.

Your final outline is now complete! Our final outline for **arctic animals** is on the next page.